W9-BNU-984

Mary Ames Mitchell

The Man in the Purple Cow House

Purple Cow House

And Other Tales of Eccentricity

The Man in the Purple Cow House

And Other Tales of Eccentricity

MARY AMES MITCHELL

HOPE
Publishing House
PASADENA, CALIFORNIA

Most of the information, names, characters, places and incidents are the product of the author's memory or the memories of her friends and family, and are represented to the best of their ability. In some cases names have been purposefully changed to protect a person's identity.

HOPE PUBLISHING HOUSE
Copyright ©2005 by Mary Ames Mitchell

All rights reserved under International and Pan-American Copyright Conventions. Published in the United States by Hope Publishing House, Pasadena, California. For information address: Hope Publishing House, P.O. Box 60008, Pasadena, CA 91116 - U.S.A., Tel: (626) 792-6123 / Fax: (626) 792-2121, E-mail: hopepub@sbcglobal.net, Web site: http://www.hope-pub.com

Library of Congress Cataloging-in-Publication Data

Mitchell, Mary Ames, 1951-
    The man in the purple cow house and other tales of eccentricity / by Mary Ames Mitchell.
        p. cm.
    ISBN-13: 978-1-932717-04-4 (alk. paper)
    ISBN-10: 1-932717-04-8 (alk. paper)
    1. Ames, Thomas Winter, 1922-1991. 2. Eccentrics and eccentricities—California—Biography. 3. Mitchell, Mary Ames, 1951- 4. Fathers and daughters—California. 5. Homeless men—California—Biography. 6. Homelessness—California. 7. California—Biography. I. Title. CT
    CT9991.A44M57 2005
    920.02--dc22
                            2005011148

This book is dedicated to my children
Jonathan Stuart
and
Amy Claire
who never met this grandfather.

CONTENTS

Ask, and it shall be given you;
seek, and ye shall find;
knock, and it shall be opened unto you:
—Matthew 7:7

My family — Tommy, Mom, Charlie, Dad and me — 1960

CHAPTER ONE

One Door Opens
Another Door Shuts

At exactly midnight on July 16, 1979, at the Huntington Hospital in Pasadena, California, I gave birth to my father's first grandchild. My son was born literally half one day and half the next. His head crowned at 23:58 p.m. on Monday and the rest of him joined the world on Tuesday. I'd been in labor for twenty-two hours and thirty-three minutes without anesthetic – natural childbirth being the latest fad subscribed to by my peers who had all been hippies, smoking pot for breakfast a mere five years earlier.

After watching the nurses clean my son and count his toes, taking him in my arms and holding him to my breast to see if he'd nurse (he wouldn't) and confirming with my husband that we'd name him Jonathan, it was agreed that my husband would call our list of friends and family while I lost consciousness.

When I woke in my hospital bed a few hours later, daylight surrounded me and cleared my thinking. Remembering the thrill of the night before at the miracle of this incredible birth, I wanted my husband to celebrate with me, but when he walked into the room, instead of the adoration I expected for all the hard work I'd just done, he plopped down on the side of my bed with an aggravated sigh. "I just called your dad to tell him about Jonathan," he said. "He didn't even wait to hear about the birth before he started yelling at me – going on and on about how you and I were part of some conspiracy. He must have just learned we gave money to that development company that purchased his building last month. He kept saying over and over, 'You two are in cahoots with those developers.'"

"But we were just trying to help him! The money was for him, not for the developers," I said.

"I know. I know. I tried to explain it to him, but he wouldn't listen. He talked right over me and said, 'You just tell Mary I don't ever want either of you to talk to me again.' Then he said if you want to contact him, you have to go through his attorney. What a nut case!"

I was twenty-eight years old. But I'd been aware for a long time my father was teetering on a loss of mental balance. Increasingly he was becoming overly agitated about what seemed like trivia to me. There was no figuring him out. He'd been happy and cheerful enough when I was little, but now he was usually angry – and impossible to please. When I was a teenager I put a lot of energy into placating him and tried all kinds of tactics: Maybe if I spoke more quickly I could keep his attention longer? Maybe if I didn't tell him about my problems, he would stop worrying so much? Maybe if I were a better person and did everything perfectly, he would feel better and be happy again? Nothing had worked then, and apparently I was forever going to disappoint him.

I had just participated in this awesome event. I'd given him a grandchild. Why wasn't he rushing over to tell me how proud he was? Why was he choosing this moment to go off the deep end? I felt a strange, sickening mixture of emotions. I was surprised, hurt and angry. I was also relieved. He was being so unreasonable that I knew there was nothing more I could do. To hell with him, I thought, and as I'd done many times in the past, I gritted my teeth, put on my cheerleader smile and resolved not to need a father any more.

The Big House — 1951

CHAPTER TWO

———◆———

The Purple Cow House

I, too, was born in the wee hours of the morning at the Huntington Hospital. During the first six months of my life I slept in a wicker basket perched on a clothes bureau at the end of the studio apartment my father had built over his greenery business in east Pasadena. From the pictures I've seen, the studio was a large room furnished with some modern furniture of the fifties and antiques inherited from Dad's grandmother that were hundreds of years old. "Your father finished constructing the studio just in time for our marriage," Mom told me. "He couldn't wait to get his grandmother's antiques out of storage and set them up in the apartment. It was very comfortable."

Eleven months after they moved in, I was born. Just before I would have been able to crawl out of that basket, a large Italianate mansion on the other side of town came on the market. In an older residential area just south of the Huntington Hospital, the house had twenty-three rooms, about 15,000 square feet and crowned the top of over two well-manicured acres. All around were similar houses built by the same architect, principally known for his design of the Tournament of Roses' house which quarters the club that organizes the yearly Rose Parade.

A small amount of money my mother had inherited when her mother died many years earlier must have been burning a great big hole in my father's pocket. For $30,000, my parents bought the house. Mind you, we did not live a life-style that required, or could easily support, a mansion. Dad made little income from running the greenery and Mom's volunteer work cost money instead of making it. "It was part of our plan to have six children." Mom told me later. I think it was part of Dad's plan to be someone he thought he was, but wasn't.

Not only did this mansion come with a lifetime guarantee to be a maintenance nightmare, but for only an extra $1,000 they could get it three-quarters filled with furniture. The scale of this furniture was so oversize, it would not fit in a house of normal dimensions. "By adding the little bit of furniture we had in our studio apartment, we were able to move right in and look reasonably at home there," Mom said.

On the front of our Christmas card that year, she pasted a black-and-white photo of herself and Dad standing in front of the ornate arched doorway of what my family came to call the "Big House." Mom wears a dark suit with white piping and proper black-and-white spectator pumps. In her arms she cradles baby me. Dad stands beside us, almost a foot taller than Mom, in the suit and tie he wore at their wedding and which he would wear again twenty-three years later at my wedding. Two white Bedlington terriers sit at our feet, one looking up at my father expectantly. As I look at that photo on the piano in my living room today in its silver frame, I think, "If I didn't know better, I'd say it looked like a Pasadena version of Camelot."

The Big House, on the corner of El Molino Avenue and Woodland Road, was built in 1924 for an Arizona cattle baron named Henry Boice. He called the house Fernbrook and when he died, it was put up for sale. The couples who'd waited for World War II to end before having their babies were busily going about creating the Baby Boom. Most of these new parents had little money and the privations of war rationing had taught them to be frugal. They were looking for homes of a more practical size and price than the Big House – like the ranch-style houses with three bedrooms, two baths and a den selling for $9,000 in a housing tract on the east side of Pasadena called Hastings Ranch by real estate agents, but nicknamed Stork Hill by Dad's contemporaries.

The Big House was a white elephant, left over from a bygone era when waiters wearing white gloves served oysters at the nearby Huntington Hotel to my great grandparents – long before the Depression changed everything. Though only a moment in history to me, my mother-in-law blamed the Depression for all her problems, just as children today blame their parents for all their problems. Baby Boom parents remembered the hunger, anxiety and dramatic losses they had just survived. No one was ready, yet, to risk having so much to lose again.

My aunt told me that in Pasadena after World War II there was a great sense of community, equality and togetherness among the young people returning home from overseas. Why would a couple want to live all by themselves in a Big House surrounded by all that space when they could be together in a tight little suburb among others just like them?

In the Big House we led what seemed a normal life – at first. Dad continued his business selling indoor plants to local retailers from his greenery. At the end of the summer of 1952, my brother was born, christened Thomas Winter Ames, Jr. after his father by family tradition. A California Institute of Technology student lived in the servants' quarters off the kitchen and helped to take care of Tommy and me when our parents were busy. The Caltech student also mowed the two acres of lawn.

Mom and some of her friends organized a charity group called the Crown Guild which held large fund-raising parties in the formal ballroom in the basement of our house and small tea parties in the glass-walled conservatory. "It's funny how the house gave us prestige," Mom said. "For the first tea party, I needed a tea strainer. So I called the local jeweler to order one. When the sales lady at the jewelry store confirmed the tea strainer was in stock, I asked if she would arrange to have it delivered. 'We don't usually do deliveries,' the sales lady responded. 'Where do you live?' When I gave her our address, the tone in her voice changed and she said, 'Um, certainly, Mrs. Ames. We'd be happy to deliver your purchase.'"

But that was the extent to which the house helped Mom in high society. Her application to become a member of the prestigious Valley Hunt Club would soon be denied.

Dad's original intention for the property was to subdivide it and sell the extra lots, using the profits to stay and live in the Big House. The position of the house on the property allowed for an easy division. When Dad tried to obtain the necessary permits, he met resistance from city officials as well as the neighbors. They wanted the neighborhood to retain its grandeur with the large lots.

I was too little to remember all this, but my mother kept a scrapbook of the newspaper articles which chronicled the events over the next eleven years. In an effort to stop Dad's plans, the city and neighbors cited the zoning regulations for single-family residences in that part of town, even though there were several other areas in Pasadena experiencing similar transitions. When Dad did his own research, he discovered the lady next door was breaking those regulations.

Mrs. Arline Kraft rented out several of her rooms to non-family members, technically making her house a multi-family residence. With Dad's sense of fairness aroused, he demanded that City Hall enforce the zoning regulation for single families on all his neighbors. Though he could have sent a letter, he chose to send a telegram – in those days they were commonly used for special messages. Inexpensive and hand delivered, telegrams were preferred for congratulatory notes after a wedding or birth, for example.

Dad's telegram addressed to Seth Miller, Pasadena Board of Directors, City Hall read, "WE REQUEST YOU AS OAK KNOLL REPRESENTATIVE FILE FORMAL CHARGES ON BEHALF OF PROPERTY OWNERS AGAINST ARLINE KRAFT FOR REPEATED VIOLATION OF CITY ZONING LAWS STOP"

"Action didn't happen quickly enough for your father, which really got his dander up," said Mom. "So he plotted to get attention another way. While he was researching the zoning requirements for our area, he'd discovered an antiquated allowance for farm animals permitted on our property. With what he considered a sense of humor, he decided to take advantage of that grant.

"He and his brother, your Uncle Bobby, who must have been about twenty-five at the time, were high school chums of the owner of the local Driftwood Dairy. One of his dairy cows was pregnant and therefore temporarily out of work. Your father and Bobby invited this cow for a pleasant holiday visit at the Big House. The afternoon they brought the cow home, I was giving a baby shower for your Aunt Kay, Bobby's wife. The young men led the mooing cow up to the window. Suddenly, there she was, peering in on my guests."

The headline of the March 2, 1953, *Pasadena Star News* read, "Highbrow Cow Stirs Society Feud," and in smaller type, "Mama Bossie Causes Fuss on El Molino." The photo shows our mansion and the mansion next door owned by Mrs. Kraft.

"The newspapers christened her Bossy," said Mom. "Her name was really number 1-0-6. The local Girl Scout troop earned their dairy badges by grooming her every day. We had a lot of fun with that cow. In fact, our neighbors Gretchen and Mel Threlkeld wrote an invitation in the form of a Western Union telegram to your dad and me for a martini which read,

'HOW NOW BROWN MOO

GRAZING ON THE AVENOO

WE HOPE YOU REALLY ARE A COW

OR WE'LL HAVE TO SWITCH FROM MARTINIS NOW

MAY WE BRING OVER A THREE LEGGED STOOL

AND JOIN THE RURAL MILKING POOL.'

"It started a long-term friendship between us," she continued. "When I showed the telegram to the papers in an effort to let them know some neighbors were on our side, they published the poem with the headline "Bovine Battle Goes From Bad to Verse."

On March 3 another article reported that animal-rights activists claimed Dad was mistreating Bossy. Yet the photo shows Bossy with a full bowl of hay under a beautiful oak tree with a wreath of white flowers around her head. Dr. Ivan Petersen, a veterinarian, stands next to her giving her a pat. The headline said, "Inhumane Plea Fails in Cow Feud."

Mom told me that on the following morning Dad answered a knock on the door to find a kind-looking Pasadena policeman. "Good Day, Mr. Ames," he said, "I've been sent by the city of Pasadena to take immediate possession of your cow, because we have been told that she has no shelter."

"That's not true," said my father. "We have built her a beautiful shelter. Would you like to see it?" Whereupon, my mother and father led the policeman down the hill to the tree where Bossy was tied. Pointing to a canvas cover he had just erected the previous day, Dad said, "See, a home built for a queen."

Sighing with relief, the policeman said, "Thank goodness, I didn't know how I was going to fit a cow into my black and white."

The headline from the paper that day read, "City Officials Take Dim View of Ritzy Feud, Say Canvas Not a Proper Cow Home."

The next day, when Dad went outside to give Bossy her morning hay, he found her back covered with purple ink as if a bottle of it had been dumped upside down from a distance over her shoulder. "The ink was apparently splashed on her between the rounds of special protection which officers yesterday promised would be given to keep Pasadena's newly famous cow from being unduly molested by pranksters." said the *Star News*.

Another newsman must have seen Bossy before Dad found her, because his headline read, "Now She's a Purple Cow." He was probably familiar with the poem written in 1896 by Gelett Burgess who'd died in 1951:

> *I never saw a purple cow*
> *I never hope to see one;*
> *But I can tell you, anyhow,*
> *I'd rather see than be one.*

Thenceforth, the Big House was known by Pasadenans as *The Purple Cow House*. Just recently I met an elderly man who, when he found out I had grown up in Pasadena, asked who my father was. When I told him, he said, "Oh, yes, of The Purple Cow House."

Dad and Mrs. Kraft declared war. At first they merely dragged each other in and out of court. Dad won the first round. The newspaper headlines read, "Bossy winner in Ritzy Feud," "Society Cow Licks the Foe," "Bows to Bossy, Widow Steps Down Out of Mansion," with photos of Mrs. Kraft temporarily moving out of her house.

Two weeks later, terrorists entered the scene and the war turned dangerous as well as ugly. Mom was having a luncheon of the Scripps College Alumnae in one of the living rooms when the meal was disrupted by a deafening blast. A four-inch pipe filled with black powder to make a bomb had been lit and tossed into a terra-cotta urn flanking the entrance to the terrace about fifty feet from the house. It smashed the four-foot vase into fist-sized fragments. The police said it was lucky all the ladies had been inside, because if they had been anywhere near the bomb, they would have been killed. Though materials for making the bomb were found in a paper bag on a nearby corner and taken into police headquarters for investigation, no one ever discovered who planted it.

Dad found out that a small arsenal of fourteen rifles was reported stolen from the Kraft's garage. "I don't know what's going on over there," he was reported as saying, "but I intend to be ready." He put an ad in the newspaper for a cannon which read, "In desperate need of small short-range cannon or field-piece artillery plus supply ammunition. Write 619 Woodland Road, Pasadena."

When a newspaper reporter interviewed Dad about the ad, he told him, "In view of the inadequate police protection we're getting here, I'm going to mount this cannon in our front yard to protect our property rights." The police told him there was no law against owning artillery as long as it wasn't concealed. Dad answered he didn't intend to conceal it.

The following week Mrs. Kraft moved back into her house and

the war became hand-to-hand combat. It appears my father initiated the new round of attacks. The paper reported that "Mrs. Kraft, an heiress to an Eastern fortune, said, 'I was quietly watering the drive when Ames drove the short distance from his place, walked up to me and roared, 'Can't your rich father afford a gardener?' Then he wrenched the hose from my hand, turned it on me, and gave me such a thorough soaking I thought I'd get pneumonia before I could get into fresh dry clothes. He first grabbed my arms and pinioned them. I was afraid of what he might do, so I fought back, got hold of the nozzle, and turned the water into his face. He let go, and I doused him with water and chased him off my place."

With the smell of the pipe bomb still in the air, and the chill between the Big House and our neighbor, my parents decided to move us out of the Big House temporarily until things calmed down.

The Sierra Madre House, 1950s

CHAPTER THREE

From Mansion to Cottage

I was three and Tommy was just over a year in 1953 when we moved out of the Big House. For $12,000 my parents had bought a very small Victorian house in the neighboring town, Sierra Madre. Nearly the whole building could have fit in the front hallway of the Big House.

Before tempers in our home or at city hall had a chance to quiet down, Dad created a new issue. He couldn't digest the fact that we were paying taxes on a large house we weren't living in. Taxes, to him, were associated with the Devil, and the big bad city was the Devil incarnate. Dad claimed the city prevented him from being able to sell the Big House by not changing the zoning laws and therefore the least they could do was lower the assessed value of the house to cut his tax bill.

When his request was denied, Dad sued the city, insisting on representing himself. He declared in a court hearing that his only choice was to abandon the property and let it decay. In that way the house would lower itself into a lesser assessment category. His plan worked. The deputy assessor showed up the next day, rechecked the property and declared the plumbing was in bad shape, bad enough to allow my father his precious tax cut.

My mother assumed Dad would eventually finish fighting and move us back into the Big House. However, neither of those things ever happened. Like an old wooden boat that an owner fusses with but never sails, the house sat on its hill without a family in it and Dad spent his weekends puttering there. Bit by bit it began to fall apart.

One night in 1954, juveniles broke in, ripped an oil painting in the drawing room, tore down window shades and a chandelier, splashed shoe polish around an upstairs bedroom, and broke some glass windows. Instead of fixing the windows, Dad hammered boards of plywood over the openings. The lawn wasn't mowed regularly, the paint chipped off the plaster portico and after a few months the property was so run-down that neighbors sued Dad for unsightliness.

In December the neighbors won their suit and the municipal court fined Dad $300 and three years' probation for allowing quantities of dead shrubbery and rubbish to collect on the grounds, creating a fire hazard. Dad filed for a mistrial, pointing back at the neighbors, saying conditions elsewhere were worse. A newspaper headline read "Purple Cow Ghost Plagues City Hall." His appeal was denied. So he sent a letter to the Department of Justice of the State of California with his complaint, without result.

He tried again that year to change the zoning law and again his plea was denied. A year later, he went to court once again to oversee a pending threat by the city to inspect the property. "Planners Ask Eyesore Elimination" read the newspaper. One neighbor claimed, "It's an insult to Pasadena." On that occasion Dad hired an attorney.

When that tactic failed he tried a new one, propaganda. He didn't like the reports printed by the local newspaper, so to plead his cause he typed up his own two-page journal on legal-sized paper and had copies made, naming it *The Oak Knoll Ostrich, A Minority Report*. He circulated it around the neighborhood by walking from door to door, placing a copy on each doorstep, but the neighbors found his attitude so unpleasant, no one wanted to side with him, even if he was right.

Meanwhile, one June evening when Mom wasn't pasting newspaper articles in the Big House Scrapbook, she and Dad made love. I learned later it was the very last time. So in March of 1955, baby Charlie was born. "As soon as I brought your new brother home, your father told me I wasn't allowed to have any more children," she said. That was the end of her dream for six children.

———•———

This isn't to say Dad wasn't a good father. In fact, he was as passionate about being a dad as he was about thwarting Pasadena's zoning laws. He was possibly more caring and attentive than most fathers I've known. Every evening, he returned home from his greenery at five o'clock, excited to find my brothers and me and see what we were up to. He was aware of what was important to each of us, asking questions about school, our day and what we were playing. He tumbled with us on the living room floor, allowing my brothers and me to climb on top of him and think we'd pinned him down so he couldn't move. Then he'd cry, "Mercy, mercy," and leave us in giggles. He seemed stronger than an ox, causing me to feel safe and protected. I knew when he was around no one would get hurt.

Often he'd sit alone and read his paper, or putter in the garden, but it would never bother him if I interrupted. He didn't travel away on business trips and our family was never required to move to another town because a corporation wanted us to. He didn't waste away in front of television watching football games or disappear to play golf or hide in a garage doing something with the door shut. He was always glad to see me.

Dad was a project person with countless plans and activities under way at any given time. He was continuously improving the house, which seemed as organic as our garden, by building new rooms. As one neared completion, another started to form. He did most of the construction himself, pouring concrete foundations, installing plumbing and electric lines. The new foundation squares were like stepping-stones to the next project. I don't remember a time when anything looked finished and, though it bothered my mother, it didn't me, especially since, between his own projects, he built a playhouse for me and a tree house for my brothers.

As one of Dad's friends said, we were, "land poor." Dad valued real estate more than fancy clothes or the latest model car. Every extra penny went into purchasing another piece of property, including several residences near us in Sierra Madre, which he fixed up and rented out.

When he drove his rounds on Saturday mornings to "inspect the lower forty" he often took one or all of his children with him. It was a treat to go to the Big House. While he fussed over plants or tinkered with the plumbing, we played in the house as if it were a museum with no guards. Most of the rooms still contained the oversized furniture now covered with dust cloths. Downstairs in the ballroom, Dad laid out a Lionel train set which extended the full length of the polished wood dance floor.

We children chased each other up and down the double stairway and played hide-and-seek in the bedrooms where there was a secret tunnel between two of the rooms. A small door in the back of one of the closets hid the entrance to the tunnel's passageway so we had to crawl through a two-foot tunnel to emerge in the closet of the next room, reminding me of C.S. Lewis' story, *The Lion, the Witch and the Wardrobe*.

The bathrooms, tiled from floor to ceiling with tiny white six-sided tiles, were bigger than my kitchen is today. One of the showerheads was quite avant-garde for its time. A large chrome ring circled the tub, like the curved rod that holds a shower curtain. It wasn't until Tommy was about six that it occurred to him to step into the tub and turn it on. We could hear the old pipes rumble as the water surged up to the bathroom, then drenched him from small waterspouts circling 360 degrees around him.

Off the hall to the ballroom in the basement was a walk-in safe some ten feet square. Fortunately, none of us were foolish enough to try locking the others inside during a hide-and-seek game. "The wife of the baron stored her fur coats in there," Dad said. Another, smaller safe was hidden upstairs behind a secret panel in a sweater cabinet in one of the closets. The cabinet was just low enough for us kids to reach so we could pull out the panel, but I never knew how Dad figured out it was there originally. Its large steel combination lock had been sealed shut long before we lived there. "Maybe the baroness left her jewels in there and when she died the combination was lost," he said. We pictured a pile of pearls, diamonds and gold necklaces inside like pirates' treasure in a cave.

My parents hired an older retired couple, Mr. and Mrs. Wallace, to live in the house as caretakers. They occupied the three-room servants' apartment over the kitchen where the Caltech student once lived. I often followed Mrs. Wallace around in the kitchen and in many ways she filled the role of a grandmother to me – in a way I certainly never experienced with my own: the full cookie jar and the home smell of baking. Mr. Wallace was usually out tinkering with his Oldsmobile in the garage built to house four cars. Above the garage was another apartment originally built for a chauffeur, now empty.

To me, as a child, the house was endless. There were two full-sized living rooms. "Did we use all those rooms when we lived there?" I once asked Mom.

"No, we only furnished one of the living rooms, leaving the other bare."

"How did the cattle baron choose which living room to use each night?" I asked.

"During the baron's era, the men retired after dinner to smoke in one parlor, and the ladies broke off to gossip in the other," she said.

I liked it when Dad took me alone with him to the Big House on Saturdays without my brothers. Sometimes while he watered the plants he tried to teach me their names – split-leaf philodendron and dieffenbachia. Other times while he was busy, I jumped rope, drew myself a grid for a hopscotch game on the sidewalk or wandered around the small sitting garden pretending I was a princess. On summer days when he hosed the dirt and leaves off the driveway, I loved the smell of steaming water cooling off the hot pavement, and also how this felt under my bare feet.

*Charlie, Tommy and me in the back yard of
the Sierra Madre house, around 1957*

CHAPTER FOUR

Sierra Madre in the 1950s

Soon after Charlie was born, we got our first television. It was black and white. Technicolor was in common use, but a color TV still cost more money than a new car. My parents carried the heavy box with its glass picture tubes into our small den, Mom at one end, Dad at the other, walking backwards. "Look what the cat brought home!" Dad shouted as he kicked open the double doors off the patio with a loud thwack. The springs on the screen screeched as he pressed his back against it, allowing Mom to carry in her end.

Tommy and I were allowed to watch cartoons on Saturday mornings. My favorite shows were *Betty Boop* and *Popeye*. Sunday nights, my parents insisted we sit as a family to watch *The Twentieth Century* narrated by Walter Cronkite. I wasn't very excited about history then, and for a long time I believed everything that happened in the twentieth century before I was born had occurred in black and white.

It seemed to me that half the TV shows were about cowboys

and Indians: the *Roy Rogers and Dale Evans Show*, *Lone Ranger with Tonto and Silver*, *Zorro* and *Bonanza*. One day Tommy and I were acting out the *Roy Rogers and Dale Evans Show* by riding our stick horses around the perimeter of our kidney-shaped garden singing, "Happy trails to you, until we meet again" as Roy and Dale did at the end of each show. We were wearing the cowboy and cowgirl outfits with real leather fringe Mom had sewn for us.

Our stick horses were made of stuffed vinyl horse's heads stuck on the end of a long pole like a broom handle with two plastic reins attached to the stick around the neck of the horsehead. We held the reins in our hands, holding the stick up between our legs as we tried to walk like a horse. As Tommy and I pranced by Dad, who was pulling weeds in a nearby flower bed, we waved and sang as if we were in the Rose Parade.

On the second pass Dad got up from his knees with a concerned look on his face and walked over to me, grabbing the plastic reins out of my hands. "You aren't holding the reins correctly," he said. By then I knew better than to respond with something like, "What are you talking about, Dad? These are just stick horses," for he probably would have yelled at me in his growly, scolding voice, "Don't you dare talk back to me, young lady." So I meekly stood there as he explained, "You aren't supposed to hold one rein in each hand. Hold the two reins together in your left hand, with the ends trailing over your hand and down on your left side, freeing your right hand to twirl a lasso or pat the rump of your horse."

"Oh," I said again, trying to figure out what he meant, but not accomplishing it quickly enough for him.

"Here, let me show you," he said, opening my fist and re-arranging the reins properly. "There. It's better to set the habits right at the beginning."

By the time Charlie was three and old enough to participate

in our games, Tommy and I, ages six and seven, had replaced the cowboy theme with another TV favorite, *Tarzan*. Mom bought leopard-printed cotton fabric and sewed a new set of costumes so Tommy could be Tarzan wearing leopard-spotted shorts and I be Jane in a one-shouldered bathing suit.

Tommy was the self-appointed stage director and alternately determined whether Charlie was cast as Boy, wearing his own leopard shorts, or Cheetah, for which he dressed in the monkey costume our grandfather had bought him one year for Halloween. The three of us climbed in and around the avocado trees lining the back of our yard, pretending we were in the deepest jungle in Africa.

The tree house was in the largest of the avocado trees and to help us out, Dad tied a heavy rope to a branch over the tree house to serve as Tarzan's swinging vine. Where the rope hung down to the ground he tied a fat knot on which we could sit or stand. "Here, I'll show you," he said, holding onto the rope with both hands and jumping up so that his feet landed, one on each side of the knot. He took a couple of circular swings then jumped back down onto the dirt. "Now, watch as I use it to climb up to the tree house," he said. Holding the rope again tightly with both hands, he began to walk up the side of the tree with his feet like a pirate climbing the side of a ship, until, with a grunt, he pulled himself into the tree house.

"Now you need a lagoon," he declared, marching off to fetch a shovel. After a couple of hours, he had dug a two-foot-deep hole under the tree and then filled it with water from the garden hose. Tommy begged to be the first to swing on the rope over the lagoon. Standing on the edge of the tree house and holding tightly to the rope, he jumped yelling "Ahheeeeaahhh" as he splashed ceremoniously into the muddy water in the hole.

The playhouse Dad built me was actually larger and stronger than the huts our Pilgrim ancestors built for their first winter in Plymouth. There were wooden bunks in one corner and I received the rest of the furnishings as presents for the next few Christmases and birthdays, including a toy stove and refrigerator, plastic dishes and doll beds. Mom taught me how to make the curtains – the first of many sewing lessons. My girlfriends and I camped there at night while my brothers slept in the tree house.

We socialized frequently with other families. Some we knew through the coöperative nursery school held a picnic at Lacy Park annually. There Dad either organized a game of catch or pushed us on the swings. We also belonged to a swimming club called Gerrishes where my brothers and I earned our Red Cross swimming badges. During the free-swim periods, Dad would jump in and play with us while Mom watched by the side of the pool so she wouldn't get her hair wet. She only went to the hairdresser's once a week and she wanted to protect her poofy hairdo which women in the fifties could not create on their own.

Early on New Year's Day, we went to the Rose Parade with other friends who had children. My parents carried two ladders and a board, one parent at each end, looking as if they were a painting crew. Dad would place the board between the two upright ladders to give our family a private bleacher looking over the standing crowd.

Dad was very creative setting up for parties when he and Mom entertained. Once he brought home a huge flat zinc planter from the greenery, some four inches deep, six feet long and three feet wide which he cleaned thoroughly with a hose in the back yard. He then set the stage for an elegant buffet fit for the Huntington Hotel by filling the planter with crushed ice – which he leveled with the same tool he used to smooth concrete.

Both my parents sang as they worked – like the seven dwarves. Sometimes Mom played Broadway musicals from her collection of 33-RPM records while she cooked. Dad often scooped me up while Deborah Kerr and Yul Brynner sang "Shall We Dance" swinging me in a polka around the room.

In an effort to pass their love of music to their children, they sent me to piano lessons, while Tommy learned to play the clarinet and Charlie blasted our neighbors with the trumpet. The half-hour daily practice sessions were strictly enforced before dinner.

Our whole family worked together to present puppet shows, complete with lighting, sound and stage effects. For many years we collected hand puppets. One Christmas, Dad built a triptych theater large enough to stand upright and hide the five of us. Mom sewed the curtains and together we painted the backgrounds that hung on poles between the two side panels. Mom helped us children write the scripts and taped our voices on a large tape recorder. Then we performed for neighbors and grandparents. The theater was also the stage for some of our biggest arguments as kids, but that probably taught us something, too.

Even going to a movie was a special occasion, saved for warm summer nights when we piled into our spacious blue Ford sedan and drove to a drive-in theater in Monrovia, some twenty minutes east of Sierra Madre. Mom and Dad sat in the front while we three kids disputed our territorial rights in the back. Bucket seats wouldn't come into fashion for another fifteen years, seat belts were rare and no one had dreamed of car seats for babies.

Dad parked the car in a spot as close to the screen as possible, then rolled down the window, released the speaker from the sound box on top of a pole by our car and hooked it over the edge of our car window. He dialed the knob at the bottom of the speaker up and down to make sure the sound worked. The movies didn't start until after dark and there was always a double feature with a break in the middle that meant we would be up late, a treat in itself. Before piling into the car, we dressed in our flannel pajamas, washed our faces and brushed our teeth in case someone fell asleep before we got home.

In between the double features, we'd walk to the concession stand just to stretch our legs, but we knew Dad wouldn't buy food at the theater because their prices were too high. Besides, we didn't eat between meals – it was a family rule – but it was fun to watch the crowd milling about and I can still remember the feel of walking on spilt popcorn with my soft rubber-soled pajamas.

My father doted on our dog, Tony, a white Bedlington terrier whom he had registered with the American Kennel Club as Antoinette d'Hiver. Hiver is French for Winter, Dad's mother's maiden name, giving Tony an official place on the ancestral tree. Tony slept in a four-by-four-foot hut Dad built her, complete with its own landscaped running yard at the side of the house. He washed Tony on Saturdays and showed me how to brush her hair until she was a puffball of soft white fur. Then we walked her together down our street and back. I could tell Tony knew how pretty she looked because of how proudly she pranced.

Few dogs and cats were neutered in those days, so most pet owners expected several litters of puppies or kittens, but Dad would only allow Tony to mate with another Bedlington. When Tony was in heat, a floppy-eared beagle that lived two doors down from us sat in front of our house at night howling. Dad periodically ran out, yelling like a banshee to scare him away. Even though the beagle consistently returned, Dad won the battle and arranged for Tony to be with one of her own kind.

My brothers and I were very excited when Tony got pregnant and the wait for the puppies' due date was harder than waiting for Christmas. Finally the big evening came. Dad was outside helping Tony when Mom made me go to bed. I could hardly sleep in anticipation of waking the next morning to find out how many puppies we had, hold them and smell that puppy smell. When I came expectantly into the breakfast room I found my Dad hunched over the table crying. I'd never seen him cry before and never would again. My little girl's heart broke seeing my usually strong six-foot-one father weep. The puppies had all died.

Usually our vacations were to the beach, but for Easter break during my sixth grade, Dad took us to Sante Fe to meet his Aunt Rosemary and another old aunt on his mother's side named Edith. Edith was ninety-plus, the oldest relative I ever met.

As Dad was tying the last suitcase to the car rack, he called me over and asked me to do something which I thought was odd at the time. "You know those old dolls you have that you never play with any more?"

"You mean the ones in the storage box at the foot of my bed?"

"Yes. Go get a couple of them and bring them out here."

I ran to my room and picked out two I didn't play with because they had no matching clothes or doll furniture and returned to the car, handing them to Dad. He didn't explain, but just smiled, wrapped them in newspaper and tucked them into the back of the car between the suitcases.

A few days later I figured out the objective of the trip wasn't so much visiting the old ladies, but rather the side excursions we made to see the Indian reservations. Arriving at the first reservation, we saw a family of Indians standing by the road, including a bedraggled-looking girl about my age. Dad stopped the car and looked over his shoulder and whispered to me in the back seat, "Get one of those old dolls out that you brought, okay?" I picked a particularly big one, then Dad told me to get out of the car with him. We walked up to the Indian family and I knew what Dad wanted me to do. I stepped towards the little girl and gave her the doll.

I'll never forget the look of surprise and pleasure on her face and long wondered how Dad knew to think ahead of such a thing.

Tommy, Charlie and me around 1958

CHAPTER FIVE

Discipline and Small Towns

My father often talked about our Puritan ancestry, so recently I studied up on those religious rebels and found that, indeed, the Puritans and Dad were much alike. It seems the Puritans liked sticking their noses in other people's business. There was actually a law in Plymouth requiring neighbors to monitor other neighbors, watching for "idleness and other evils occasioned thereby and to require an account of them how they live." Like Dad, the Puritans wanted freedom to express their own beliefs, but were intolerant of those who differed from them, and their striving for perfection meant they were highly judgmental of everybody else.

On the other hand, Dad inherited some good values. I never saw him cheat, steal or tell a lie. Life in our house in Sierra Madre was run with Dad's strict Puritanical discipline, a control he couldn't impose in his vendetta against the city. He didn't build stocks in our front yard to enforce the rules, but my brothers and I knew he would correct us only once. If we didn't stop misbehaving immediately, we were in for either a booming order to go to our rooms or a spanking.

Spanking was considered normal punishment in those days, but Dad only spanked me once. I must have been very small because I don't remember what I did to deserve it, but it was the last time I got in that much trouble. It's one of those experiences I don't remember not remembering. I'll never forget the whap, whap, whap of his strong, broad hand which left my tiny fanny burning red. I winced when I stood up, pulled up my panties and hung my head in shame. My soul felt empty and a weight of pain crushed my chest. For me, that event accomplished its goal – I knew who was the boss in our house.

The town of Sierra Madre had a built-in orderliness. We lived for a decade in this small, tight-knit community until I was thirteen. Bordered to the north by the massive San Gabriel mountains, it sat on the edge of the foothills, slanting down to the flat lands of the San Gabriel Valley. At night from the window by my bed I looked out over a sea of twinkling lights – Pasadena sleeping below. When I was very small, I thought the lights were angels.

Our town's main street, Sierra Madre Boulevard, sliced through the middle of the village paralleling the edge of the foothills. Along that street we did our marketing, visited the library and dropped off our laundry. Shops were not open on Sundays because it was still God's day and no restaurants came to town until 1963 because most people still cooked their own meals and ate at home together.

Our street, Ramona Avenue, ran parallel to the boulevard two blocks down the hill. Sierra Madre Elementary School, which I attended from kindergarten to sixth grade, was two blocks up the hill. On my walk to school, I passed the fire station in the middle of town where at precisely noon every day a loud horn blasted like a sonic boom, announcing the arrival of the lunch hour.

Next to the fire station was the central park where my Brownie troop met after school. Across from the park was the gray-stone Congregational church where I attended Sunday school. Every evening at five, the bells in the Romanesque tower played the Evensong – the signal I was to stop whatever I was doing and go home to get ready for supper. That's also when Dad arrived and he wanted me there when he got home.

Meals were similarly predictable. We sat down together for every meal in the same seats. Dad sat at the east end of the table, Mom at the west end, Charlie and Tommy on the south side looking through the kitchen to our garden and the mountains. I sat on the north side looking across our street and over the same view I had from my bedroom window.

For dinner, Mom placed five warmed plates in front of her seat with the hot dishes full of food spread in a semi-circle around the stack. The rule was that the oldest woman and guests were served first. The youngest male, usually Charlie, was served second to last and finally Mom served herself. We were required to wait until she finished serving and picked up her fork before we could begin eating. We did not say grace. We could not have dessert unless we finished the food on our plate. This was a problem when Mom served peas, which I hated, until I learned to spit them in my paper napkin when no one was looking and ask if I could be excused for a moment to go to the bathroom.

We were never given anything unless we said "please" at the end of our request. "No manners, no merchandise." We had to ask to be excused before we were allowed to leave the table. When we were excused, we were required to push our chair in before we could run away to play – and we knew the rule was firm: never any eating between meals.

Probably because my parents each grew up with servants

who served meals on punctual schedules, our eating schedule was precise. Breakfast at seven, lunch at half-past twelve and dinner at six. Breakfasts were so regimented you'd have thought a programmed robot was cooking in the kitchen instead of my English mother. Monday through Friday mornings I found one egg, either scrambled or poached, one piece of buttered toast, and a small glass of orange juice placed in front of me. Dad received two eggs and two pieces of toast. We never had cereal because it didn't contain protein.

At Sunday breakfast, we three children fought over the two sheets of the funny papers, while Dad read the rest of the *Pasadena Star News* at the table. We didn't talk much. If my parents wanted to talk about something they didn't want us children to know about, they spoke French. Saturdays we ate lunch at home and Mom usually served a cup of Campbell's soup with a sandwich and one glass of milk. My favorite soup was split pea because she cut a hot dog into little slices like pennies and floated them on top.

For dinner, Mom made sure three colors were represented on the plate – a white starch, green or yellow vegetable and the meat. A little more of her English childhood showed up when she made meat pies. Steak-and-kidney pie was her signature dish and tasty when the steak pieces outnumbered the kidney pieces.

All this orderliness existed side-by-side with Dad's extramural battles. But, from my vantage point, our lives were as normal as could be.

One Saturday morning when I was seven, I saw someone whose life was totally different from ours. Dad and I were driving home from doing errands and going to the Big House to water the lawn. As we reached one of the two intersections in town with traffic lights, Dad brought the car to a stop on the red. While we waited for the light to change, a dirty unshaven man wearing a jacket so worn you couldn't tell what the fabric was made of, walked in front of our car in the crosswalk. His shoulders were slumped, his hair wild and unkempt and his stomach stuck out like a soccer ball.

I had never seen a homeless person before, not even a drunk, though I had heard about *hobos* in stories who snatched free rides on trains, walked bow-legged, lived under bridges and traveled with all their belongings tied up in a red-and-white handkerchief tied to the end of a stick carried over their shoulder.

Dad still had vivid memories of the Depression so he was more accustomed to this sight than I was, but for some reason that moment was burned on my memory and I never forgot Dad watching the man stumble in front of our car and then saying, more to himself than to me, "Boy, has that man seen better days! Guess he's pretty down on his luck."

Me, Dad, Tommy and Charlie by the ferry on Catalina Island

———

CHAPTER SIX

Take a Trip
1959

When I was young, I had no idea my parents weren't happy in their marriage. I assumed Dad cuddled with Mom while twirling the curls at the nape of her neck, told her she was beautiful and soothed the worry wrinkles from her forehead as she fell asleep, as he often did to me. I never saw Mom ridicule Dad for his causes, or realize, as I do now, that she has always turned her back on anyone who shows any emotion. I didn't understand that in her past she'd been so hurt by loved ones whom she didn't please, she expected the same mistreatment from her husband. These stresses didn't become clear to me until I started putting the pieces together for this story. "Your father started withholding affection from me on our honeymoon," Mom told me recently.

I wasn't the only one shielded from their tensions. Dad probably never told anyone and Mom didn't spill her marital woes to her father, a professional psychologist, until the eighth year of their marriage. Then my grandfather's advice to my mother was his solution to all problems: "Take a trip."

My mother's family suffers from a genetic affliction known by us as the Hopkins Travel Bug. Every year my grandfather Hopkins took a two-month trip. When my mother finally confided in him, he'd just spent a month in Egypt, followed by visits to Persia, Ceylon and then India. When he died in 1972, his obituary reported he'd traveled to nearly every country in the world.

His parents, Mary and Charles Hopkins, also traveled extensively, circling the world a number of times. Now that I've delved into the family history I realize this bug has been in our blood for a very long time. It was recently discovered that when our ancestor Stephen Hopkins left England on the *Mayflower* in 1620, it wasn't the first time he'd set sail for the other side of the Atlantic. Eleven years before, he'd boarded a ship heading to Jamestown that was wrecked on the way in Barbados. He and the crew built another ship and finally reached Jamestown. Stephen then traveled around the New World for several years seeing the sights before returning home. Since his wife had died while he was gone, he remarried. When he learned that passages were for sale on the *Mayflower* heading back to Virginia, he purchased seven – for himself, his new and pregnant wife, three children and two servants.

I suppose that's why travel was so important to my mom's grandparents they set up a special trust fund for Mom and her siblings to be used for one purpose only – travel. Mom's father knew about this trust and wrote a letter to his banker, as if he were writing a prescription for medicine, giving the banker permission to give Mom money for five tickets to Europe for a family junket. When the banker called my mother to tell her what was happening, it took him a while to convince her that the trust did indeed exist, for this was the first she'd heard about it. "Take the trust fund out for a spin," he suggested. "You are the oldest child. Use it. Someone has to set the precedent."

ly mother sat down for a chat with my father. "I think it
ld be good for us to take a trip to Europe together." she said.
"How will we do that?"

"Evidently one of the trust funds my grandparents set up was
for travel purposes. Dad has given us permission to use it."

Realizing the full potential of the situation, my father said he'd
go, but only if we stayed for a full six months. This was more time
than Mom had in mind. I was seven, Tommy was six and Charlie
was only three. Since it meant taking my brothers and me out of
school for the last four months of the term, Mom had some difficult organizing to do, but she pulled it off. "I was extremely glad
I let your father have his way once again," she said. "It was one of
the most wonderful times in my life."

As it was for me.

Dad was as happy as a honeybee in a lavender patch planning the trip, choosing the places we would go and what we'd
do. It had been fourteen years since V-E Day when his youngest
brother Bobby had been in Italy flying fighter planes and his older
brother Bud had been with the army in the Pacific. Dad, who'd
stayed Stateside during the war, wanted to visit the places Bobby
described in his letters, so Italy became our main destination.

Soon dinner hour at 305 Ramona Avenue became *European
History 101 for Children Seven and Under*. We also began Italian
lessons. Dad set up a competition. Whoever spoke Italian the
best after the trip would get five dollars. After dinner when Mom
usually did her sewing, I watched her make two wool suits for me
with pleated skirts and matching jackets – one solid gray, the other
a hound's-tooth check of pink and green. We went to the brand-
new Sears Roebuck to pick out two white shirts with Peter Pan
collars to go with the suits, which she would hand-wash in hotel
sinks along with my brothers' and father's white shirts every night

of the trip. Wash-N-Wear and Drip-Dry fabrics were new and dryers are still rare in most of southern Europe.

We left Los Angeles International Airport on a twin-engine propeller plane headed to New York City nonstop. That was a big deal then and took about nine hours. Tommy, Charlie and I were the only children on the plane. I didn't stay in my seat much, preferring to hang out with the stewardesses more than with my fussy brothers. The stewardesses kept me busy fetching things for passengers and answering calls for coffee refills. No liability laws prevented a little girl from helping in those days.

As our taxi drove into New York City, I saw skyscrapers for the first time and was amazed anyone could be up so high, building anything. We stayed for several days visiting the normal tourist sites. At the Empire State Building, the tallest building in the world at the time, the elevator ride up was very exciting, but I was disappointed when I stood on the platform at the top to discover I couldn't see the whole world.

What impressed me most about our hotel were the new synthetic carpets. My brothers and I discovered that by shuffling around, we gained static electricity and could zap each other with a tiny spark. We spent hours shuffling and zapping each other like human bumper cars.

Finally we each repacked our brown Samsonite suitcases and took a taxi to the pier where our Italian ocean liner, the *Augustus*, was waiting. Walking out of the embarkation building, seeing the ship looming above us, was as exciting as the first time I entered Sleeping Beauty's Castle at Disneyland. Even better was knowing we wouldn't have to leave for home at sunset, which would have been the case at Disneyland back then. The gangplank loomed high above the ocean. The narrow halls were jammed with people looking for their staterooms. The ship's horns were booming. I was thrilled.

As we sailed out of the harbor, the Statue of Liberty seemed small compared to the huge expanse of open ocean beyond. I thought we were sailing into a never-ending sky. I didn't understand the concept of the earth's curvature and found it hard to believe that Genoa, our destination port, was somewhere out there ahead of us.

The *Augustus* was to be our home for a week, and by the end of the first day, we were comfortable with finding our way around the ship. The March air was still too cold for swimming in the deck pool, so to pass the time, I explored every corridor within the restrictions of third class on my own. There was no fear of letting children wander about without their parents. I looked into corners, watched other passengers and tried to imagine what the rich people were like upstairs in first class.

I made friends with an Italian sailor who played shuffleboard with me and tried to improve my Italian. I admired the enameled pin he wore to keep his kerchief straight, so at the end of the trip he gave it to me and I still have it in my memory box under my bed. He was the first to nickname me "La Biondina." In Italy there were few fair-haired children.

On the second day everyone in my family got seasick except me. When I went to fetch my sweater in the cabin, the four of them lay in bunk beds, groaning. My jealous brothers growled at me to keep quiet. It was a rare treat to see my brothers miserable. I skipped off gleefully to find my sailor.

At night we participated in activities with our parents. Dinners were long sit-down affairs where we had to practice our manners. One night, Dad ordered the fish soup, looked at me and said, "There's something very different about this soup." When the waiter placed the flat European-style bowl in front of him,

Dad nudged me in the arm to look at his soup. There I saw a tiny purple and black sucker-covered tentacle from an octopus. To me, an octopus was only something that appeared in movies, large monsters that ate submarines, though *A Voyage To the Bottom of the Sea* wasn't released until two years later. Dad's eyes giggled as he opened his mouth wide and spooned in the soup. The curly tentacle disappeared in between his lips, like a fly just captured by a frog. I yelped, "Dad, you didn't really eat that!"

"Yum," he said.

After dinner, sometimes bingo was set up in the dining hall and our family shared one card. My brothers and I took turns putting the marker in the *Free* space and filling in the squares, hoping to be the lucky one to jump in the air and yell, "Bingo." Other nights, the dining room was transformed into a dance hall and Dad tried to teach me the waltz and the foxtrot. He'd count out the one-two-three, or one-two-three-four. I tried hard not to step on his feet, which seemed to take up the whole dance floor. I looked up as he held me around the waist, and I stretched my right arm high to put my hand in his palm. He was so tall. I leaned my head against his tight stomach, feeling how strong he was. When the dance was a polka, it took me a few tumbles to get the rhythm, then we whirled around and around and around the dance floor, laughing and trying not to bump into anyone.

On the last day, when I knew we were nearing land, I stood next to Dad at the polished wooden railing peering at the uninterrupted horizon we had seen for so many days. For as hard as I squinted, trying to see a lump or a shadow, most of the morning nothing appeared. Suddenly Dad pointed and there it was – the Rock of Gibraltar. My box-shaped Brownie camera was waiting in my hands. I used all eight exposures.

Dad had prepped us well. We knew the Rock meant we were

entering the Mediterranean Sea – that oval puddle of water the boot of Italy stepped in and that we would be in the port of Genoa soon. As the ship eased into the bustling port we were greeted by small wooden motor craft piled with white lace and red and green linens which muscular, suntanned men tried to sell us, making their offers in Italian, now a familiar sound.

We disembarked and headed for our next destination, the beautiful fishing village of Santa Marguerita, a short distance south of Genoa. It's on the same small peninsula as the village of Portofino on the Ligurian coast, otherwise known as the Italian Riviera. We checked into our hotel, thinking we would soon find a place to rent and stay for several months, but the weather was colder than my parents expected. So instead we repacked our suit-cases and piled onto a train bound for the southern seaside town of Sorrento on the Bay of Naples.

The front lawn of our hotel in Sorrento extended to the edge of the seawall overlooking the bay. To our right we could see the tangle of cranes and docks in the seaport of Naples with Mount Vesuvius hovering in the background like a dunce cap. Dad told us how Mount Vesuvius blasted its top off, covering the Roman city of Pompeii with volcanic ash and burying Herculaneum in molten lava. As I stared at the volcano, I imagined a drift of smoke coming out of its top.

When we visited the excavated Pompeii a few days later I was awe-struck by the plaster figurines of men, women and children crouched by the side of the roads where there had been pockets left in the ash. When Vesuvius erupted, the ash had covered every-thing with twelve feet of hot cinders, instantly incinerating the people there. Where there once were bodies, bubbles of gas formed, leaving human-shaped holes in the ash which the excavators filled with plaster. When the lava was taken away, graphic statues of the victims were revealed – like stone ghosts from the past acting out the event. Some statues were looking back over their shoulders in panic as they saw the cloud of ash coming towards them. Others were covering their eyes and heads to avoid it. Later in the '60s when people tried to imagine what a nuclear holocaust would be like, I thought of those statues in Pompeii.

Dad wanted to look closer inside the mouth of the dragon that caused all this destruction, so we took a tram to the top of Mount Vesuvius, climbing straight up the side of the barren, gray mountain. When the tram stopped, we stepped out on the edge, overlooking the round crater, but all we could see at the bottom of the bowl was a smoldering puddle of boiling mud.

The next day back in Sorrento Dad bought some fishing hooks and line wrapped around red plastic reels. That afternoon on the dock of our hotel he conducted his Drop-Fishing Class for the three of us. The water was so clear I could see a baby octopus crawling from under a rock as I unwound my line down to it. When the little fellow actually ate my bait I sat there in disbelief, which was a good thing because it gave the hook a chance to set inside his mouth.

"Bring it up, Signorina," said a hotel steward who'd been standing there watching me. I did, but once the slimy, mushy lump was hanging like nothing so much as a limp, gray heap from my hook over the dock, I didn't know what to do with it. So I handed it to the steward. When he asked me if I wanted him to take it to the kitchen, I didn't dare tell him no. I didn't realize what I had done until that night in the dining room, when the same steward picked up the silver dome covering my dinner plate. I caught Dad laughing at me when I discovered the delicious taste of frito misto.

For the people of Europe in 1959, the memory of World War II was still fresh. Old women dressed in mourners' black because most of them were either widows or had sons who had died in the war. What affected me most were the beggars who congregated around all the tourist attractions, begging for a pittance so they could eke out an existence. Tiny, orphaned urchins with dirty faces, torn clothing and calloused, unshod feet often surrounded us in the markets. When we left churches, we walked through aisles of ragged, wounded veterans. Legless men were strapped to wheeled platforms, pushing themselves along the street with filthy hands. Others, with no arms, leaned on battered crutches, the empty shirt sleeve tied up with a piece of string as if it were a duffle bag. As hungry hands reached toward my face I wanted to cry. Unlike most of the children I grew up with back in California who would vote for Nixon and Reagan, I was coming face to face with war's real meaning.

The weather finally warmed up enough for us to return to Santa Marguerita. Nestled in two precious coves of the rocky Riviera, this is still my favorite town in the whole world. My parents rented a two-bedroom flat on one of the three floors of a pink building with a nice courtyard aptly called the Villa Rosie. An Italian family with three young boys lived in the flat below us. Their mama, Maria, taught Mom how to cook Italian dishes so we were soon eating spaghetti, cannelloni and lasagna just like our neighbors.

For the three months left in the school year, Tommy and I were enrolled in a private Catholic school a short walk away. Dressed in a black smock, white plastic collar and bright-colored plaid bow, I found myself at a wooden desk with an ink well in which to dip the pen I used to write Italian words in my composition book.

As summer approached, Dad looked for a place to swim in the Mediterranean on weekends, not an easy task along that rocky coastline. Some local residents told us about a nook between Santa Marguerita and Portofino with a sliver of rocks, no sand, just big enough for a dozen people to rest their towels and beach bags while frolicking in the water. We named it Rocky Parragie after the real Parragie – an expensive, private cove around the next bend in the road which had covered cabañas for dressing.

While Mom sat on a towel on a rock, keeping her hair dry and knitting mohair sweaters with wide collars like Jacqueline Kennedy was wearing those days, Dad swam with us – frolicking with us in the water and standing legs spread apart so we could swim through them like a tunnel. He also bought rafts on which we floated, chased one another and inspected the tidal pools. He seldom rested on the beach unless there was someone he could talk to – aside from Mom.

He'd bought one of the snug, black bikinis worn by Italian men. Though this fit in with the local fashion, he looked funny to me. At home the custom for beach wear was loose shorts in Hawaiian prints called *baggies*. I wasn't used to seeing my father wearing something revealing the shape of his private parts so publicly. Besides, he didn't look Italian – he was bigger with fair skin and freckles.

A young bachelor in town named Giorgio befriended our family and often spent the day at Rocky Parragie with us. My brothers and I loved to ride on the back of his Vespa scooter. Our home movie of the trip shows us with our arms around his waist, holding on for dear life, as he swerved in and out of the curvy road between Santa Marguerita and Portofino. The movie also caught Giorgio hiding under a towel, trying to change his clothes on the exposed beach.

One night he and my parents threw a cioppino party at our apartment. My brothers and I were put to bed early, but we could hear guests arriving with lots of laughter, talking in Italian and bringing sea food to drop into the pot – langostino, local mussels, octopus and whatever white fish they were able to catch or buy that day. I smelled the simmering stew on the stove while falling asleep, happy to hear my parents enjoying themselves.

However, my parents weren't getting along as well as I imagined. One day shortly after the party, Mom announced she was going to Rome for a week. She would take my baby brother Charlie with her, but Tommy and I would stay behind in Santa Marguerita with Dad. There were no questions asked and no reasons given. Decades later Mom admitted to me, "Your father and I had a fight, I can't remember about what, but I needed to get away to cool off."

When school ended in June, we prepared to leave Santa Marguerita to spend the last two months of our trip seeing the rest of Europe. Dad promised we'd see Venice where the streets were rivers and people rode in gondolas instead of cars. Then we'd see the snow-covered Alps of Switzerland where cuckoo clocks were made. In France we'd visit real castles surrounded by moats and in Holland we'd see windmills. A ferry would take us to England where our mother was born and where Big Ben loomed over the Thames. Finally we'd visit Scotland where men wore skirts.

The weekend before we were to leave, Mom and Dad left my brothers and me with Maria downstairs and traveled by train to the Fiat factory in Torino, returning with a brand-new blue and beige Fiat 320 Multipla which looked like a Volkswagen bus but was only half the size. We would spend up to eight hours a day in it for the rest of the trip. We came to feel safe and sound in this home away from home.

On the second day in our hotel in Venice, Dad pulled me aside and whispered, "I want to take you on a secret errand without your brothers." I agreed eagerly because I'd have done anything to have him all to myself. Holding hands, we walked through tiny alleyways for several blocks, crossing over canals on narrow bridges. He led me to a section of town crowded with jewelry stores, to the window of a shop he had been to. My nose just reached the bottom ledge, so I looked straight onto a sea of gold rings, bracelets, medallions and earrings. I was dazzled.

"I want you to pick something out for yourself," he said, first explaining the difference between fourteen- and eighteen-karat gold.

I was so excited. Everything looked pretty, but what most caught my eye were gold gondola brooches in various sizes. We went inside the store and I pointed to the one I wanted. It was small, only about a half inch long. The saleslady polished it in a soft cloth and placed it in a square gray velvet box. As we walked home, I felt as if I had all of Marco Polo's riches in my pocket.

Though we visited way too many castles and cathedrals, there was one castle my brothers and I particularly liked. In the middle of its extensive gardens was a maze created out of six-foot high boxwood hedges. The leafy walls formed concentric circles leading to a stone tower in the center. While my brothers played tag among the alleys of the maze, I tried to find my way to the tower.

Finally, after a number of dead ends, I found the center. I ran up the circular stairway inside the tower and came out on the round balcony on top. As I glanced around me, I heard my father's deep voice from below. "Rapunzel, Rapunzel, let down your hair." I looked down below to see him at the base of the tower, grinning up at me. I had short hair, but I pictured myself untying long blonde braids and releasing my hair to flow to his hands so he could climb up the side of the castle, just as the prince did in the *Grimm's Fairy Tale* he had read to me so many times back home.

Long before our trip to Europe, my father loved raiding thrift shops and trash bins. He'd often stop the car to rescue Spanish tiles from a building that was being demolished or convert someone's discarded rusty tea kettle into a planter. "One man's trash is another man's treasure," he'd say. Mom shared some of this passion and in Europe our car came to a halt in front of every antique store along our path where my parents filled a bag on the rack above the car with treasures and trinkets, creating a bundle which was almost as big as the car itself.

Though six months seemed like an eternity to my eight years, we finally came to the end of our trip. From England we took a ferry back to Amsterdam. From there our car was sent to America filled with our loot on a ship that would take it through the Panama Canal and ultimately to the Los Angeles harbor. We sailed home on the *America* to New York. From there we flew to Chicago for a three-day visit with Dad's oldest brother Bud and his family whom I'd never met. Then we flew the last leg to LAX. Like a huge blue present, the car arrived several months after we were safely back in Sierra Madre. Tommy won the five dollars for learning the most Italian.

Building a beach house, Ventura, California, 1960

CHAPTER SEVEN

The Healing Ocean

Once we'd settled back into home life on Ramona Street, Dad decided to pursue a master's degree in city planning which he felt would give him a professional status to back him up when the Battle of the Big House resumed. He enrolled in a one-year course at the University of Southern California and started doing homework at night after dinner on a card table set up in the middle of the living room.

"Something happened to him at USC or he met someone that changed his life," Mom told me later. "He started coming home late after his week-night class, sometimes in the wee hours of the morning, smelling like beer and cigarettes. Since he didn't smoke, it was obvious he'd been to a bar, but when I asked him with whom, he was evasive. 'Oh, I just went out with some friends from school,' he said.

"I suspected he was having a relationship with someone whom he didn't want me to know about. Our sexual life had ended years before when I conceived Charlie. His moods became darker and then one Saturday afternoon when he claimed he was going over to water the lawn at one of our rentals, he didn't come back for dinner. So I went over there to see what was up. The house was dark and empty. We didn't have any tenants in it at the time. I walked into the living room and there he was, back in a dark corner in a fetal position, quiet as a mouse.

"'Tom, what's wrong?' I asked.

"'Nothing. Leave me alone,' he said. So I went home and made dinner for you children.

"Eventually he came back, but still wouldn't talk to me about it. I finally went to see a marriage counselor and asked your father to go with me.

"He attended the first session, but after a few minutes walked out and said he wouldn't have any part of it. The counselor then told me, 'There's nothing I can do to help your husband, Mrs. Ames. He seems a little paranoid. You'd better take care of yourself.'"

When the semester at USC ended, Dad quit the master's program. Completely ignoring the missing parts of his marriage, he brought up a subject with Mom one night that they'd discussed frequently in Santa Marguerita. "Let's build a beach house, up near Santa Barbara so we can be close to your father in the summer time." My Grandfather Hopkins, then seventy-five years old, lived alone in Santa Barbara, a two-hour drive from Pasadena.

On Saturdays or Sundays for the next several months, my brothers and I were packed into the back seat of the Fiat for the drive up the coast to a strip of beaches between Ventura and Santa Barbara. We passed orange groves that still bordered the highway and we always stayed alert for Thousand Oaks, now a sprawling suburb, but then only a horse farm with a large red barn where newborn colts wobbled or frolicked in white-fenced pastures.

Sometimes Dad knew ahead of time about a lot for sale, so we'd inspect that. Other times it seemed we drove around aimlessly until he found a lot with a "For Sale" sign on it. On the way back to Sierra Madre, Mom and Dad discussed the weather conditions, the views and other pros and cons of what we'd seen. Bored sick in the back seat, my brothers and I started dreading weekends, but at least Dad was talking about something positive, rather than his fights with the city. He was also happier, having a new project and he loved being able to spend time at the beach.

Finally my parents settled on two pieces of property within a block of each other in an area called Pierpont of Ventura. They bought both of them and developed a plan similar to what they had planned for the Big House. They would build on the lot farther from the beach, sell it, and use the proceeds to build a bigger home on the better lot facing the ocean.

In complete contrast to how Dad had conducted projects in the past, a real architect was hired, plans were drawn and approved for a modern redwood building which soon became a reality. We continued to drive to Ventura on weekends to watch the building progress. By May, it was finished and we spent a couple more weekends purchasing furniture. Finally, when school let out, we packed a summer's worth of clothing into the Fiat and drove up to stay.

During the five summers we were there, we had no television, no cell phones, no computers, no fax machine, no microwave and no PlayStation – just an RCA Victor record player and a spanking new Nu-Tone mixer that didn't sit on a pedestal like the ones we'd had, but fit into a motor built right into the kitchen counter.

Dad joined us on the weekends, driving up on Friday and home Sunday night. "If he'd been there the whole time, we would never have been able to carry off the charade of a peaceful-looking couple," Mom said. The first thing Dad did on Saturday mornings was walk down Pierpont Boulevard to the liquor store which sold newspapers and comic books. He returned with the local paper before Mom served breakfast. After we children went off to play, while Mom cleaned up, he'd stay at the table with his paper and coffee or take both out onto the sun deck.

During the rest of the day, when we weren't all at the beach, he busied himself around the house, just as he did around the Big House and the Sierra Madre house, hammering, sawing, pouring cement for a patio or puttering in the garden. Usually he accompanied this by singing Broadway tunes with a partially finished bottle of beer standing nearby.

Whether working outside, swimming, sitting on the sand or strolling along the water's edge, Dad wore that black bikini he'd brought home from Italy, only now it really looked out of place. His body was in good shape because he worked out with a set of bar bells, plus his muscles were firm from lifting plants and doing construction work. His physique was similar to that of Popeye after a good can of spinach – wide muscular shoulders, a tiny tight butt and slender, strong legs. I was happy he was in good shape, but I was even more embarrassed than ever that part of him was so clearly visible on a public beach. But I would no sooner have revealed those thoughts to anyone than cut off my own fingers.

Many of Dad's projects were artistic. The first summer he made a rubber mold of one of the marble friezes he'd purchased in Italy of three cherubs that he'd named after us: Maria, Tomaso e Carlo. He cast several copies of the frieze, pouring plaster of Paris into the mold and we loved the thrill of watching him pull the mold from the casting. Would it come out cleanly, with three perfect faces or would air have been trapped inside the mold, making pockmarks and deformities? Alas, one plaster cherub was born with no nose. Dad also made a windscreen of driftwood between the garage and the patio, incorporating the odd shapes and sizes into a pattern. When we took Tony on her morning walk at the beach, I helped Dad comb the sand for interesting wood shapes.

On sunny days Dad helped blow up canvas rafts like the ones we had at Rocky Parragie. My brothers and I dragged them to the ocean where he taught us how to catch the wave under the front tip of the raft and let the water push us to shore. Dad learned to surf as a teenager so for Christmas after Tommy turned eleven, Dad gave him a surfboard and the following summer taught him how to use it.

At first I was jealous; my younger brother had gotten a real surfboard while I was expected to continue riding a canvas raft. I'd seen the movie *Gidget* and thought being a surfer girl was cool, but when Tommy let me try it I found it awkward straddling the board with my legs spread apart and the wax scraped my knees when I paddled. From then on I was happy to stick with my canvas raft.

On overcast days, my brothers and I found other ways to amuse ourselves. We built forts under the low-hanging cypress trees by the water to play pirate games or we rode bikes to the sandy, undeveloped area past the Pierpont Center to search the desert for horny toads. The third summer we watched bulldozers dig up that sandy area as they began to create the Ventura Marina. At night we played card games. My favorite was Tripoly. Sometimes we took a picnic to the beach, roasted hot dogs on a fire made of driftwood and melted marshmallows for s'mores on the ends of coat hangers. Mom played a twelve-stringed tiple and led folksongs she'd learned in a singing group in Sierra Madre. Dad cuddled me in his arms as we stared at the stars, pointing out the Big Dipper and Orion's Belt. He would comb my hair with his fingers as he talked.

The Christmas after Tommy received a surfboard, the whole family got something even bigger. My brothers and I ran out of our rooms Christmas morning to discover an eight-foot white wooden boat balanced on its side between the wall and our tree.

"What's that?" Tommy squealed, though he knew quite well what it was.

"It's called a Sabot," said Dad. "Sabot means wooden shoe in French."

"Where'd you get it? Do we get to ride it in? Is that really for us?" we all chirped.

The Sabot spent the rest of the school year leaning against the end of our carport in Sierra Madre. We'd traded in the Fiat for a bigger car, a Chevy Nova station wagon, so in June Dad strapped the boat to the top of the car and off to Ventura we went.

The morning after we arrived was sparkling and sunny. As soon as we finished the breakfast dishes, Dad drove us to see the new marina which had just opened with a dozen rows of docks and a sprinkling of boats in the slips. It would grow much larger over time as the bulldozers continued to dig out the desert southward, along the coast.

Dad parked the Nova beside one of the new docks, attached a bow line to the Sabot and in one swift movement lifted the boat off the car and into the water. He skillfully tied the bow line around a cleat on the dock, giving it one last tug to make sure it was secure. Then he stood up, gave a satisfied sigh and said, "There! We don't want it to float away, now, do we?" After pulling the mast, sails, centerboard and rudder from the back of the station wagon he said, "Gather around me, please. We're going to learn how to make this thing work."

After demonstrating how to hoist the sail up the mast and place the rudder and centerboard correctly into their slots, he proceeded with instructions on how to figure out the direction of the wind. "Put your pointing finger into your mouths and get it all wet," he said. When three index fingers of his children were dripping with saliva he continued, "Yes, that's right. Now, stick it up into the air like this."

We held our fingers up as high as we could.

"Now, do you feel how one side is cold?"

I didn't, but I nodded my head as if I did.

"Good. That cold side is the wind. You have to know where the wind is coming from before you can sail. It's all about the wind."

I was already a failure.

One by one, he took my brothers and me out in the Sabot to teach us how to sail. He was such a large man the boat was lopsided and crowded. As he taught me about tacking, he said, "When it's time to turn the boat, the captain must yell, 'Coming about,' to make sure everyone ducks so that the boom doesn't crash into your head. Here we go, Mary. Ready? Coming about," he yelled, simultaneously pushing the tiller away from him.

I was still back on page seven, trying to figure out what "tacking" was and didn't get out of the way fast enough. "Mary, duck!" he roared, reaching towards me with an outstretched palm and forcing my head and shoulders into the bottom of the boat to escape the swinging boom. There was no room in the bottom of the boat, so I ended up crunching my mouth into his knees. When I came up again, he was looking so happy with the wind blowing in his face and our little sail full of air, I didn't want to complain and ruin everything.

My favorite beach memory is the night we went grunion hunting. Grunion are skinny silver fish about a foot long that live along the coast of Southern California and northwestern Mexico. Between February and September, on the nights with the highest tide, they scurry onto the beach with the waves, wiggle their bottoms into the sand and lay their eggs. An inner biological clock tells them every 14.8 days to ride a wave to shore. Their eggs are left behind, then after another 14.8 days, waves from the next highest tide break the eggs and take the baby grunion back out to sea. The light of the moon makes the event spectacular.

Each run lasts about an hour. After several summers in Ventura, we were accustomed to hearing residents exclaim the "grunion ran last night" as if they were saying the Easter Bunny had been here. Grunion hunting meant staying up late at night to wait on the beach, and we were always put to bed early. Dad knew how much I wanted to see a run and finally at the end of the third summer, he promised to wake me when we heard there would be one.

I was dead asleep when I felt Dad shaking my shoulder. "Honey, get up. The grunion are running." I had gone to bed fully dressed and only needed to throw on a jacket before we were dashing down the street towards the beach. We climbed over the sand dunes to a spectacular array of burning campfires lighting up the sand as far as we could see. Where the waves hit the beach, a coating of glistening fish shimmered like slippery silver spikes. Many of the fish were up on end, trying to burrow into the sand, others were just wiggling on shore on their sides where we could grab them. Dad handed me a pail as we joined our neighbors, scurrying along the water's edge plucking and cramming the grunion into the buckets before the tide took the fish back to safety.

With a friend on the beach at age thirteen

CHAPTER EIGHT

Puberty

Each summer we stayed at our beach house until the Back-to-School ads appeared in the August newspapers. As we came over the last hill at the end of our drive home, I always felt as gray as the cloud of smog we could see ahead of us, hanging over the San Gabriel Valley. Life may have seemed like a bed of gazanias during the summers, but when we returned to Sierra Madre, we entered the real world again.

Bad things were happening to the Big House the year I entered the fifth grade. Teenagers were regularly breaking windows and vandalizing it. I accompanied both parents after one incident to survey the damage. Boxes we'd stored in the basement were broken into and Mom started crying when she saw the contents of her childhood doll house smashed and thrown around as if it were chicken feed. Dad continued to board up the windows but left rubble where it was. As window by window succumbed to plywood, the place got darker and darker inside.

"Why don't we fix the Big House up and move back into it?"

I asked. "Maybe if people see we live here they will stop breaking in."

"Now you're talking just like your Goddamned mother," he said. It was the first time he'd sworn in my presence. "The city won't get off my back, but I'll lick this thing. You just wait and see."

He stopped taking care of the two-acre garden completely. The grass died. Roses became untamed brambles. A car, which he'd parked in the sitting garden where I used to pretend I was a princess, was set on fire by vandals and burned to a crispy hunk, leaving only a carcass. One day Dad rented a bulldozer and, like an angry football player, bashed the whole garden down. He uprooted the dead grass and shoveled bare dirt over my princess garden, burying the flower beds and stone-lined paths the baroness had put there. "I want to build a parking lot," he said.

What was once a sloping garden was now a bare dirt mound. The house, which had looked lonely and deserted sitting atop the lot, now looked haunted. "Why would he do that?" I asked myself. "I thought he liked beautiful things."

Pipes encrusted with dirt and rust, which previously fed a sprinkler system, now stuck out haphazardly as if more bombs had exploded. Dad asked Mom to help him pull the pipes out, but they were too heavy for her to manage. "I asked him to get another man to help him," she later told me, "but he firmly said no. When I retorted that I thought he was using the place to fight some inner battle, he turned on me, like an angry wounded predator with a face so ugly it still scares me to think about it, 'You're just like all the rest,' he said."

Dad stopped singing while he worked. Instead of playing with us when he came home at night, he went straight to his bedroom, saying, "I'm going to take a nap before dinner."

But he didn't mind if I went in to visit him. The room was dark and smelled like potting soil. "Hi, Mary. How about a back rub?" he'd say and roll over on to his stomach, waiting.

I'd throw off my tennies, if I had them on, and climb up onto the bed. I sat on his fanny, facing the back of his head and his broad shoulders. With my knees bent under me, I dug my fingers as hard as I could into the deep muscles on his back and around his neck. "Harder" he'd say. I was still small enough to stand up and walk on his back, which I did. "That's better," he said. I felt like an Italian lady pressing grapes, stomping and squishing his back with my feet in a circular motion, alternating between the shoulder area and his lower back.

———————

As I started sixth grade, most of my friends started puberty. However I had no physical signs indicating it was my turn. All the same, Dad decided it was time to make sure I didn't grow up too fast. I wanted to shave my legs like the other girls in class and stop wearing socks with my tennies. Though he forbade me that, he came into my bedroom one evening after I'd taken my bath and handed me a bottle of Johnson's Baby Oil.

"Here, rub this on your legs and it will make them shiny, as if you'd shaved them." All the baby oil did was make the hair on my legs glisten and show up more.

I hoped he would become more lenient as I prepared for seventh grade, the beginning of junior high school. I was afraid to confront him with the matter face-to-face because I was afraid he would yell at me, so I wrote a note to both my parents and left it on Dad's pillow before I went to bed.

The following morning, as I was waking up, I heard a swishing sound as Dad slipped the note back under my door. He'd written his responses to my requests in the margins. Here is the letter, with his responses underlined.

> *Dear Mom and Dad,*
>
> *These are my requests for 7th grade. Will you please talk them over carefully? If you do not agree may I have a complete answer where I understand?*
>
> *1. May I please put in as many curlers as I need as long as I do my homework first and I am in bed at 8:30 or maybe nine. O.K. if you abide.*
>
> *2. May I wear peds with my flats and shorty socks with my tennis shoes. If standard at school OK but not necessary after school.*
>
> *3. May I wear most of my dresses at the top of my knee cap? No. Fortunately styles are dropping the hem.*
>
> *4. Can I wear natural nail polish as long as I wear only one coat at a time? Number of coats not important. Naturalness is!*
>
> *Thank you*
>
> *Your ever loving daughter,*
>
> *Mary*
>
> *P.S. In 8th grade may I please go steady? No. Not in the 10th grade either.*

I was disappointed by some of his answers, but I'd won more ground than I thought I would. I wrote that letter in 1963, the year Kennedy was shot. At the time, the dress code in public schools required girls to wear skirts with hems long enough to touch the floor if we got down on our knees. The junior high assistant principal in charge of enforcing the rule that year was Miss Nelson and she was plainer and more somber than a nun! Every morning, she stood sentry outside her office watching us pass on our way to class. We new girls quickly learned from those older, experienced eighth graders that if we bent over a bit, our skirts looked longer, but if Miss Nelson suspected that our skirts were too short, she commanded us to kneel down in front of her, a humiliating experience. If the verdict was in her favor, she either sent us home from school with a suspension note or called our parents to have them bring a different skirt which gave the girls with working mothers a disadvantage.

Contrary to Dad's concern with my legs, he was eager to help me fill out the top of my bathing suit, something I couldn't do naturally. He must have noticed that during the summer between seventh and eighth grade, I covered myself up immediately with a towel or robe when I came out of the ocean so no one would see how breastless I was. The following December he took action.

By Christmas tradition we left our stockings for Santa on a hook over the fireplace before we went to bed. Santa filled the stockings and then laid them at the foot of our beds after we were asleep, so we could open them while we waited for our parents to wake up. Since there was always an orange in the stocking, we had something to eat while we waited.

My Grandfather Hopkins came to stay with us for the holidays which meant he slept in my room while I bunked with my brothers on the other side of the house. When I woke up, it took a few minutes to remember why I was in my brothers' room, but then I recalled it was Christmas. I wiggled my toes to see if there was anything at the bottom of my bed. Sure enough, my toes found something heavy and, when I wiggled them again, I heard the rustle of wrapping paper. I sat up, fetched the full stocking from my feet, and started digging.

Besides a bright-colored pencil set and headband I'd wanted, I felt something mushy on top of the orange. I pushed and squeezed this for a few seconds with the tips of my fingers before reaching in to pull out two cone shapes of foam rubber. At first I couldn't figure out what they were. Then with a sickening feeling, it dawned on me. Dad had fashioned a set of falsies for me, cutting the corners off two squares of the foam until they were shaped like breasts.

In agonized anticipation that my brothers would look down from the top bunk and see what I was holding, I quickly jammed the foam structures back into my stocking and shoved the whole package under my pillow. I lay there dreading Christmas breakfast and wondering what I could say to my father, even though I knew I wouldn't dare say anything. The healthy response would have been to laugh or maybe even scream at him and tell him what a beast he was. I wasn't that healthy.

Sure enough, when I saw Dad a little later in the living room, he gave me a grin that told me he was proud of his joke. In his mind, all he was doing was acknowledging the fact that he knew I wanted a new figure. My reaction was that I wanted a new father.

The development of my breasts and the condition of my legs weren't the only things Dad was watching. He was also obsessed with my manners. Even though we lived in a middle class neighborhood, dressed like middle class people and went to middle class schools, he did not think of his family as middle class. In his mind we were aristocrats and he set out to make an aristocratic young lady out of me.

I was sent to dance lessons with two pimply boys whose parents were also trying to climb up the social ladder. I took ballet classes to learn how to curtsy, just in case one day I was a debutante or presented to the Queen. I learned how to play tennis so I'd fit into a future social club. Dad seemed not to notice that his Purple Cow episode had already struck me off the lists of future debutantes.

Dad had rules for just about everything such as when to stand and when to sit. Dinnertime stopped being the pleasant family gathering it had been because, as chief of the manners police, he was too busy yelling at one of us to get our elbows off the table or sit up straight.

One night he was so upset he abruptly left the dining room, returning with six red lengths of plastic-coated electric wire in his hand with which he proceeded to tie the six shoulders of his three children to the ladder-backs of our dining chairs. When he finished he said, "Maybe that will get you three to remember to keep your shoulders back." I caught Mom grimacing during the struggle, but she remained silent. When I asked her later about it she said, "I didn't want to contradict your father. At the time I thought it was better not to interfere."

The worst memory I have is of the night I broke the Elbow Rule. I was sitting quietly next to Dad at dinner in my normal place, bothering no one. However, I was off in a daydream somewhere and didn't realize my elbow had found its way above the table horizon. Suddenly I caught the flash of a metal spoon as it came crashing down from my father's direction and whapped my elbow out from under me. My elbow hurt a lot, but what hurt even more was the scowl of anger, almost hatred, in his eyes when I glanced up at him in shock after he'd hit me.

My grandmother Edith

———◆———

CHAPTER NINE

Grandparents

I knew only two of my real grandparents, my mother's father and my father's mother. My other grandmother had died before I was born and though my paternal grandfather was alive and seemingly well in the Bahamas, my father had been estranged from him since World War II. He was fittingly referred to as the Mystery Man.

We could tell which of my grandparents was coming to visit for the holidays by what was on top of the refrigerator. Grandpa loved very ripe, blackened bananas. Grandma liked a grapefruit-flavored soda pop called Squirt which Dad bought by the six-pack to take the place of the alcohol he'd taken out of the liquor cabinet and hidden elsewhere. Dad's mother had been an active alcoholic until she married Dad's stepfather, whom my brothers and I called Grandpa Paul. Dad was in high school at the time. Paul warned my grandmother when he married her that if she ever took another drink he would leave her. She'd remained dry, at least to a degree that satisfied Paul. All the same, Dad didn't want any temptations left in her path.

By the time I was in the eighth grade, Grandma and Grandpa Paul lived in a retirement village in Carmel Valley, seven hours up the coast from Sierra Madre. When they visited, they drove down in their blue Thunderbird and stayed at the Eaton Inn near the Santa Anita racetrack so Grandpa Paul could spend a few afternoons betting on the horses.

I wish I could remember more about my Grandmother Edith, after whom I was named, though I dropped my first name when I got married. She left nothing written to help me, such as letters or memoirs, like most of my other relatives. She was sleek and elegant, but carried herself with a slight slouch as if she were trying to appear less tall than her shorter husband. She wore expensive-looking clothes, including kid gloves that were not at all frilly. She smelled of Pall Mall cigarettes and Chanel No. 5 and had the low voice of a smoker. She was calm, but not very cheerful. In fact, my memories of her are of a very stoic person.

We visited their home a couple times. Their apartment was as straightforward as my grandmother, decorated in light shades of yellow, in the modern style of the forties. The only thing on the cocktail table was a crystal and silver cigarette container and its matching ashtray. No lace pillows, shawls, afghans or cut-glass bowls full of candy cluttered up her space.

Grandma and Grandpa Paul spent their free time playing bridge and golf and they always had their golf bags in the trunk of the Thunderbird. In the only conversation I recall having with my grandmother, I asked her, "Do you like playing golf?"

"Yes. Why?"

"It doesn't seem like a game in which anyone is having fun, like in tennis or kickball."

"It's a good sport when you are older and retired," she said. "The way I look at it, if you spend your time doing something, why not take a long walk on the green grass of a beautiful golf course?"

She and Paul played bridge with Mom and Dad. Sometimes I sat near them and watched, amazed by how quickly and precisely my grandmother could sort her hand. Usually they played after we children went to bed but from my room I still could hear her well-manicured nails clicking on the table while she was thinking.

Grandpa Paul was a pleasant little man with no children of his own. He liked teaching my brothers and me card tricks. Once he taught me how to do a double-shuffle. He'd smoked his pipe so much that dark purple spots were developing in the corners of his lips. I didn't know then those spots were signs of trouble.

During their visit to our house at Christmas in 1964, Grandma took me shopping "downtown." I was thirteen and had never done anything with her alone before. Going downtown meant putting on a dress and gloves, leaving the heights of little Sierra Madre, and driving three miles to the Bullock's and I. Magnin shopping center in Pasadena. We ate lunch in the tea room on Bullock's second floor, with wallpaper like a garden's latticework covered in ivy. I was terrified my manners weren't good enough to please her, but she seemed happy enough with me and bought me the most beautiful linen dress I'd ever owned with an appliquéd vine of leaves, like those on the tea room wallpaper, running down one side of the front. Though it would have been the perfect outfit for that day of shopping with her, I never got another chance to wear it.

No sooner had Grandma and Grandpa Paul returned to Carmel than he was put in the hospital for jaw cancer. Half of his jaw was removed. Mom told me later that when Dad wanted us to go visit him, his mother advised him to leave the children at home. "When your father insisted, I said to him, 'Tom, don't push your mother,' but his only response was an angry stare." The five of us drove to Carmel in the Chevy Nova.

How I wished Dad had listened to both mothers. When we walked into Paul's hospital room we were greeted by his half face. His poor mouth was ugly and deformed and he was drinking his meal from a straw. We didn't stay long, nor did Paul. Two weeks later he passed away.

My parents in 1965

———◆———

CHAPTER TEN

Divorce

As I entered eighth grade, I still didn't get it that my parents' marriage was in danger. Divorces were rare in middle class families like ours, our friends' or our neighbors'. I thought only movie stars and bored rich people got divorces in those days.

I did notice Mom sometimes left the family room hurriedly while we were watching TV as if she'd forgotten to turn something off, or excused herself from the dinner table in the middle of a meal leaving Dad with a sulky look on his face, as if he'd been told he couldn't have dessert. However, she always returned several minutes later with a cheery smile. But I'd notice her red eyes and how she finished her meal without talking, looking down at her plate, which meant she was mad about something. It didn't cross my mind she was thinking of divorcing my father. Like most children, I only thought about how my parents treated me, not about how they treated each other.

Dad was such a tyrant and was angry so often I viewed it as part of the everyday course of events. I figured it was because my brothers and I were rough-housing too loudly in the back seat of the car, or that the cement in the new foundation he was building was drying too fast, or that snails were eating the leaves of his favorite dieffenbachia plant. Often I took his anger more personally, thinking I was too careless or not as smart as he thought I should be.

When Dad corrected everyone for doing things imperfectly, I assumed that's what all fathers did. When he found dust on a banister, he wrote D-U-S-T on it with his finger, leaving the message for Mom to find and fix. If his coffee was too strong he demanded she make a new pot. If the hospital corners on my bed weren't even, he'd say, "That's not right. You'd better do it again."

My brothers and I were assigned different chores around the house and Dad micro-managed all of them. Mine was to empty the trash baskets daily. I hated it, but in spite of feeling like Cinderella, I would never have complained. I dutifully fetched the large basket from the kitchen, walking from room to room, dumping smaller baskets into it before emptying the overflowing basket into the stinky metal cans stored outside at the side of the house. Sometimes I ran into spider webs or saw rats scurry away. On rainy days dirty, rancid water collected, adding to the smell of mildew and rot that always drifted around the can. If a scrap of paper was left at the bottom of a basket, I'd hear about it.

During the '50s and '60s, it was important to control your emotions, especially if your mother was English. When ours was growing up, it was considered disagreeable to complain about your lot in life, especially if you were more privileged than others, which she was. Dad was less reserved. His emotions were right there on his face and he said pretty much what he wanted to, no matter whom he deflated in the process. Even though my mother often said to me, "Mind your temper," she would never say it to him.

"Dysfunctional" wasn't a popular word yet. People who couldn't manage their lives were called "mentally ill." In the movies of the day, characters didn't dare talk about their feelings or they would end up on a psychiatrist's couch next to a shrink who was stiffly observing them from a swivel chair. It was more appropriate to salve one's unsettled emotions with a stiff martini – or three – at the end of a bad day than to have a heart-to-heart chat with a good friend. For my mom, you were either cool, calm, collected and therefore psychologically healthy or you were mentally sick.

"I couldn't talk about my marriage to my friends, anyway." Mom told me later. "They wouldn't have given me very good advice. Helen's husband Bill threw to the floor dishes of food she had made if he didn't like the way they tasted. Trudy and Harry down the street were so alcoholic they ended their evenings with fistfights."

Yet Dad's changing behavior was frightening Mom. "I thought he was crazy and if I didn't do what he wanted me to do, he would end up hurting me." This fear was encouraged by her marriage counselor. "He warned me to be ready to leave at a moment's notice if your father became unreasonably violent, so I started planning my escape. I wanted to take you back to England with me, but I knew your dad had enough money to follow me anywhere I went and I'm sure he would have."

As it turned out, her fears were overblown. Soon after Grandpa Paul died, Mom asked Dad for a divorce. She told my brothers and me one night we were leaving the Sierra Madre house but that Dad wouldn't be going with us because he was moving to the Big House. He went so quietly I didn't even notice and he even helped Mom find our new house, a four-bedroom ranch house in east Pasadena.

The Mystery Man, my grandfather
Harbour Island, Bahamas 1965

———◆———

CHAPTER ELEVEN

A Bad Year All Around

The year 1965 was a bad one for my father. Right after he'd settled back into the Big House, my mother received a call from the retirement home in Carmel telling her that my grandmother, Edith, had taken an overdose of barbiturates and died. Mom had to break the news to Dad.

Later I asked her how he reacted. "He broke down in tears. He was also very surprised. Your grandmother had been in good health and had managed to stay away from drinking while Paul was alive, but when he was recovering from his surgery, he insisted she hold his martini every night as he sipped it through a straw. It must have been too much for her because once Paul died, she evidently started drinking alone and then added the bottle of tranquillizers."

A month later, with a bizarre sense of timing, Dad's real father, the Mystery Man, entered my life. A letter to me was delivered to the mailbox of our new house in Pasadena. He'd written on engraved stationery and had an impressive address: Box No. 1,

Harbour Island. What surprised me most was hearing from this person I'd never had any communication with before, even though he was my grandfather.

Though he and Dad no longer communicated, the Mystery Man was still on speaking terms with his own brother in Chicago, who spoke to Dad's brother in Chicago, who spoke to Dad's other brother in Maryland, who spoke to Dad. Somewhere in this string of letters and phone calls, my grandfather learned about me and that my dad no longer shared a house with us.

Why he decided to strike up a relationship with his California granddaughter will remain another mystery. He never contacted any of his other grandchildren – my six cousins and two brothers – although years earlier, he'd sent a cryptic telegram to my mother when my brother Tommy was born: "BEST TO YOU AND TOM. SORRY I WAS SO SLOW IN SENDING MY CONGRATULATIONS. HOW'S BIG TOM BEARING UP UNDER THE STRAIN OF FATHERHOOD? POP. STOP." Three little lines in fifteen years.

For two months my grandfather, whose given name was Knowlton Lyman Ames but whom everyone called *Snake*, and I carried on a correspondence. His first letter had been as short as his telegram to my mother. "Hi Mary, What are you up to? Send me a photo, Grandpa."

With the second letter he enclosed a clipping of one of his articles from Harbour Island's local newspaper, *Harbour Island Nowadays*, for which he wrote a regular column and which was much chattier than his letters to me. In the paper he gossiped about who was visiting the island, who got married and who was entertaining. He also included a historical anecdote about an old sugar mill.

I thought it was funny how – like Dad – he was intrigued by local news trivia. Eventually, both men would withdraw from society, yet both would continue to be fascinated by its goings-on.

In his fifth letter, he sent me a snapshot of himself wearing Bermuda shorts, standing on a dock next to a green pick-up truck A large wallet hung out of the breast pocket of his loose shirt. Dark glasses and a Panama hat completed his ensemble. On the back of the photo he wrote, "To Mary from Grandpa Ames, Spring 1965, Harbour Island."

Two months went by without any more letters. Just as I was wondering what had happened to him, Dad received a letter from his brother Bobby with this news clipping from *Harbour Island Nowadays*.

Old Tribune Correspondent K.L. (Snake) Ames Jr., Dies
KILLED IN TRAGIC DROWNING ACCIDENT
Mr. Knowlton Lyman Ames, Jr., a long-time resident of Harbour Island, and one of the most famous personalities ever to settle here, died in a tragic drowning accident last night at the age of 68.
As was his daily custom, Mr. Ames drove down to the Government dock at Harbour Island at 5:45 last night to meet the incoming ferry bringing in passengers from the Bahamas Airways flight to North Eleuthera.
It was a very dark and rainy night, and the only other people on the dock were Mr. and Mrs. Lionel Sweeting, who were waiting for their son Bradley, who operates the ferry.
The ferry, hampered by the bad weather, was late in coming in, and Mr. Sweeting was using his car lights as a beacon to help guide the boat in.
Mr. Ames, tired of waiting, said he was going home. Mr. and Mrs. Sweeting, who were on the lookout for the ferry, paid no

more attention, although they later recalled hearing a bump.
Ten minutes later they realized they had not heard Mr. Ames
drive off, and his truck was nowhere in sight. They ran to the
edge of the dock and looked over. The truck, which was appar-
ently in reverse when Mr. Ames started off, was resting on its
back wheels in 12 feet of water, the headlights still on.
At the same time the ferry arrived with the Methodist minister
Mr. Rex Owen and Mr. Ian Malcolm of Pink Sands aboard.
They and Mr. Bradley Sweeting immediately went to Mr.
Ames' rescue and Mr. Owen applied artificial respiration until
the government doctor arrived. The doctor continued respi-
ration but after 20 minutes when there was no sign of life,
pronounced him dead.

The article included a photo of my grandfather in a different pose than in the one he sent me, but there he stood by his pick-up truck. He wore the same Bermuda shorts, the same shirt with the wallet hanging out, and the same Panama hat. It was almost as if my grandfather had sent me a picture of himself waving good-bye, before stepping into that truck and backing off the pier.

By the end of my father's forty-second year, he'd lost both real parents, a step-parent, gotten divorced and gone to live by himself in a house with twenty-three rooms and all but a few windows boarded up.

Front hallway of the Big House

CHAPTER TWELVE

The Haunted House

By the time Dad moved into the Big House, he must have felt as stripped of glory as the house was. The teenagers who'd been getting their thrills trespassing on the property realized someone had moved in and a rumor spread the house was haunted. This brought more pests than before. Dad prepared for another war.

In an old pile of toys in the basement, he found a BB gun. It no longer worked, so was harmless, but it served his purpose. When he heard teenagers playing in the yard at night, he ran into the dark and yelled, scaring them away with the silhouette of the gun.

I was unaware of all this until one night, visiting with friends from junior high school, the older brother of the girl at whose house we were, arrived home with a carload of fellow football players from the high school. They were all excited about their latest escapade at a haunted house where an old man lived. One of them described it, "We snuck up to the mansion and all of a sudden he popped out from a bush where he was hiding and came out after us. He had a gun and he chased us and threatened to call the police, but Harry was waiting in the car with the motor running and we got away."

"Where is that house?" someone asked.

"It's that big, old boarded-up thing on Woodland Road and El Molino, down there by the Huntington," another answered.

Mortified, I tried to hide in the shadow of a friend sitting next to me and prayed, "Please don't let anyone know this is my dad they're talking about." Fortunately, nobody seemed to make the connection.

When the divorce was settled, Mom paid Dad off for his half of the Big House. California was a community property state, and both their names had been on the deed. Dad used the money to buy another house close to Mom's, leaving the Big House completely vacant again. A few months later, Mom woke me up in the middle of the night, "Mary, I have to leave for a little while. The Big House is on fire. Will you be all right?"

By the next morning all that was left of the mansion was the smoldering foundation. The police told Mom an arsonist had started the fire in three places. Dad blamed Mom, saying she wanted the insurance money. Mom blamed Dad for letting the place get so run-down. I'll never know how it burned down, I just remember hoping my dad would go back to normal with the house out of the way.

———◆———

When my son Jonathan was born twenty years later, I lived in a house just a few blocks from the lot where the Big House had been and became friends with an older couple who lived kitty-corner to that property and remembered my father. "Your dad did a very kind thing one day when he was living there," they told me.

"One day the daughter of the rector from All Saints Episcopal Church who lived across the street was hit by a car near the corner. Your dad called the paramedics and stayed with the injured girl until they arrived. I think the rector owes the life of his daughter to your father."

During those intervening years, nothing had been done to the property except take away the safety hazards. Six families in the neighborhood combined to purchase the land from my mother, but could never agree on a plan for it. Trees were overgrown with partly broken branches hanging from them like the limbs of wounded soldiers. Weeds encroached on what was left of the asphalt driveway. Soon the memory of the grand house faded from the collective memory – or almost.

One morning, as I was working on the flower patch in my front yard, a young couple came strolling down the sidewalk. I'd noticed them standing in front of a scraggly house several doors down from mine; it was badly in need of landscaping, painting and new roofing, even though underneath it was a cute cottage. It tended to attract people who like to fix things. The couple noticed me in the middle of my flower bed and stopped to ask, "Is that house down there for sale? It doesn't look like anyone lives there."

"No," I said, "an elderly lady lives there who is perfectly content with the house the way it is. She's just a little eccentric, and thinks weeds are beautiful."

The couple laughed and then she said, "That reminds me of the real haunted house in Pasadena. Do you remember that huge, old falling-down place that used to be on the corner of Woodland Road and El Molino? We used to love driving by it as teenagers."

The apartment building at the end of Chautauqua Boulevard heading towards Santa Monica beach

CHAPTER THIRTEEN

Leaving Pasadena

It upset my mother when Dad bought a house so close to hers. He thought he was making it easier for my brothers and me to walk to his house after school. Mom thought he was stalking her. My older brother Tommy and I would have preferred that Dad move farther away because he was not much fun to be with. All he wanted to talk about were his grievances with our mother. He also embarrassed us when he picked us up at school dressed in raggedy jeans and crumpled tee shirts. They were often sprinkled with potting soil and sometimes steer manure from tending his plants. He looked more like a field-hand than a middle class father. And though he was never drunk, he always smelled of beer.

Charlie, unhappy about attending sixth grade at a new school, felt sorry for Dad. He could see how unhappy he was, too, and tried much harder than we did to please him. Dad used this lever and appealed to the court again, asking for custody of Charlie. The situation got dramatic one day when Charlie walked home from school earlier than usual. Mom had been dating a doctor who happened to be our pediatrician. They'd been swimming in our pool that afternoon and gotten carried away, taking their love-making to the nearest bedroom, a room detached from the house with a separate door which was Charlie's new room.

When Charlie reached home, he went straight to his room where he found our mother in the heat of passion with his pediatrician. Charlie made an about-face and ran lickety-split down the street to Dad's house. With fuel added to his cause, Dad asked for an immediate court hearing.

All three of us children were asked to appear and testify about our mother and the doctor. I was pulled out of school the day I was supposed to try out for a part in a school play. My brothers and I waited with Dad in the hallway of the court building as I watched my watch, hoping we could get our testimony over with so I could return to school for the audition. It wasn't until late afternoon that the judge threw out Dad's request for my brothers and me to testify, but by then I'd missed my chances for the play.

Luckily, when Dad received the inheritance from his mother's estate, he decided to move to Santa Monica. He still had a good eye for real estate and he was happiest at the beach. When a twenty-eight-unit apartment house went up for sale on the corner of Chautauqua Boulevard and Pacific Coast Highway for $100,000, he bought it.

Dad on the balcony of the Mezzanine overlooking
Pacific Coast Highway

———•———

CHAPTER FOURTEEN

A New Castle

The salt air seemed to breathe life back into my dad. Being directly across the highway from Santa Monica's popular public beach meant the front apartments of his new building had a million-dollar view overlooking the ocean and a wide expanse of sand. At sixteen I had little appreciation for what looked to me like a pretty run-down operation.

Built in the '30s, the ground floor of the building had been constructed for retail use and had housed a market with a high, exposed-beam ceiling. Directly above the market, but below the two floors of apartments, was an irregularly-shaped room used for market supplies. Oddly, the storage room had the only access to the building's only balcony but the door and nearby windows to it were boarded over with plywood. One of the first things Dad did after he moved in was rip off the plywood which had been covering the best view in the house for over thirty years. Standing on this balcony, you saw the Santa Monica Pier to the left and the Pacific Coast Highway curving its way along the coastline towards

Malibu on the right. On rare, clear days you could see Catalina Island dead ahead.

Dad christened the storage room the *Mezzanine* and with wood and appliances rescued from salvage yards, he created a loft with three tiny cubicles for his three medium-sized children, like the small dressing rooms of a photographer's studio. He thought if each of us had a private place of our own, we would want to visit him more often. The walls of each cubicle were of unfinished plywood, seemingly anchored to nothing. Mine enclosed me in a cocoon barely big enough for my twin-sized bed, but not for a dresser. No two walls were the same height. No edge joined any other edge.

My brothers and I stayed with Dad every other weekend. My mother had bought me a car on my sixteenth birthday, so I drove us there, parking in a triangular lot at the back of the property. On summer days, beach goers would have paid dearly for that parking spot. I liked going to the ocean so it was an incentive for visiting.

One Sunday morning as I was waking up in my cubicle, I heard Dad shuffling around the apartment, busy as usual. It was barely light enough to see anything, but I knew he had been up long before dawn. His rustle came closer, my door creaked and his head peeked inside my box. He knew I often woke early, too.

"Mary?" he said. Even his whisper had always had a low gravelly sound to it. "Can I talk you into some breakfast?"

Leaving quietly so we wouldn't wake my brothers, we walked south on the sidewalk dividing the beach from Pacific Coast Highway for a quarter mile. With the crashing waves in the background, we could smell the seaweed with each gust of warm wind as we walked. Where the buildings crowded to the edge of the highway leaving no sidewalk, we crossed to the other side and walked between the speeding cars and the cliff on a tiny strip of land, hardly wide enough to go single file until we reached the spot where Wilshire Boulevard finishes its stretch from LA to the Pacific Ocean. Hiking up a slope from the beach to the plateau of Santa Monica at the top of the cliff, we walked along Wilshire some eight blocks to Lincoln and our destination, the locals' coffee shop called Norm's. We'd walked a good mile, but since it was too hard for Dad to talk over the highway noise, most of the trip was made in peaceful silence.

Sitting in the same seat at the same counter where he sat each morning, Dad sipped two or three cups of coffee with cream, reading most of the front page and real-estate section of the *Los Angeles Times*. He chatted all the while with me, the waitresses and other early customers about city politics and the weather. If a stranger should sit nearby, he'd ask them where they were from or why they were in California. When he could, he slipped in references to movie stars and Hollywood, two of his favorite topics.

Finally satisfied with his fill of coffee and local gossip he said, "Shall we head back? Those brothers of yours ought to be waking up about now." This time we took the back way home, staying on top of the plateau, and walking along palm-lined Ocean Avenue, parallel to the highway and coastline below. The vista there, as the sun brightened, was beautiful. When we reached the Chautauqua canyon we descended down to the beach along a narrow alley which wiggled us back and forth along the edge of the cliff to sea level.

We were in a quiet valley there, so as we walked, Dad began to chat, venting his opinions on the condition of his neighborhood. "Those people put their sprinklers in yesterday, but they're too close to the house. The plaster will rot," he declared, as if I owned a home myself, and needed advice about planting my garden.

As we got closer to the intersection by his building he said,

"I have written the city three times about how dangerous that crossing is. When are they going to replace that road sign? You can't even see it because of that sharp curve there." His voice began heating up as he spoke about these things. I understood he considered the mile between his apartment building and Norm's to be his turf, and felt it was his job to make things better, but these outbursts were making me uncomfortable. His emotions seemed to be getting out of control, and his complaints were about trivial matters. To change the subject, I brought up my tall, fair and adorable, though religious, boyfriend Rick.

"We are going to a retreat next weekend with Rick's parents' church." I said.

"Has Rick finally talked you into being a Baptist?" Dad asked with a twinkle in his eye. He knew he was lucky to have a teenage daughter whose boyfriend wouldn't dare lay his hands on her. He also knew I knew he thought people who went to the Baptist church were "a bunch of phoney baloneys."

I tried again to change the subject and brought up my upcoming cheerleader tryouts. But he had advice about those as well. "You know, you should practice on softer ground, not the hard pavement, to protect your feet." Next I tried asking if he liked my new sweater. "Well, turtlenecks are a bit unbecoming on you. You should stick to blouses with a scoop collar to show off your long neck and nice shoulders."

In a way I was grateful my father even noticed these personal details, because my mother would not have. She wanted my company, but seldom asked questions about my school work, my friends, how I dressed or my activities. "You bring home B's so I don't worry about you," she'd say. She often discouraged my friendships because they took me away from spending time with her. I believed she was even jealous of the dog Dad had given me when

I turned fourteen, right after the divorce, because one day when I came home from school, she announced she'd had the dog put to sleep for seemingly no reason.

I tried hard to get my parents' attention. I won the cheerleader tryouts as well as the competition to be one of six pom-pom girls the following year. Most of the students in my high school of 3,600 would watch me perform cheers and dances at the games each week, but never were either of my parents among those in the bleachers. Nonetheless, Dad gave me advice on nearly everything. Though I found this level of interest annoying, at least it was better than no interest at all.

As we reached Dad's apartment building, something else grabbed his attention. "Oh, look at all those food wrappers those hitchhikers left out in front of my place," he said. "I could shoot them for that."

I was relieved to no longer be the focus of his critical observations, analysis and running commentary. But I was left to wonder how easily he could switch off what to me was an interactive conversation. He found an old gum package more interesting than I. As I was left holding the conversational bag, I was reminded once again that my father was not normal.

My great great great great great grandfather
Lieutenant Colonel Thomas Knowlton
Hartford, Connecticut, 2005

CHAPTER FIFTEEN

Being Different

By now I was giving up all hope my father could be normal. In fact sometimes, though I knew it was silly and pointless, I fantasized about having the type of dad who came home at night from a real office, wearing a business suit and wanting one of those stiff martinis, instead of a beer. I imagined that sort of father wouldn't get upset by little things like street trash.

It wasn't until many years later, after a study of our family history, that I understood Dad could never comply in such a way. The family legacy was a stern resolve against any compromise of principles and it was instilled in him as deeply and as early as the Elbow Rule.

A quick tour through the gallery of Dad's ancestors shows the standard up to which he tried to live. The very name by which they were often known by the Establishment in England says it all: Nonconformists.

Since the days his forebears helped colonize New England, they'd been leaders and forerunners. They'd left behind friends, family and their homeland in *Olde* England so they could practice their religious faith the way they wanted to. They'd created a nation out of what they felt was nothing, and they'd fought, sometimes to the death, in wars to keep this country and their rights here. Usually this meant going against great odds. Dad assumed he was as special as they'd been and was as determined to stand up for what he thought was right, too.

In the way my Mom's family was influenced by the Travel Bug, Dad's family was directed by the Salmon Gene. My nickname for my son is *My Little Salmon* because he always wants to swim against the current. Just as bird dogs intrinsically love to fetch and sheep dogs love to herd, so my dad and his relatives love to kick against things that look like barriers.

Looking back as recently as Dad's grandparents, one can see how this tendency became ingrained. His mother's father, Thomas Winter, after whom he was named, was the most recent immigrant. He'd been the eighteenth child born to the mayor of Grantham in Lincolnshire on England's eastern side. Grantham's claim to fame was as the birthplace of Isaac Newton and – much later – of Margaret Thatcher.

Thomas was only three when his father died, and as the youngest, he stood no chance of an inheritance in the 1800s. Still he was able to pay for a university education in San Malo, France before leaving the shores of Europe alone for Canada in 1879. The steamer which brought him would have taken a month to cross the Atlantic. He scouted with the Mounted Police, participating in the last Indian uprising in British Columbia. In 1891, he migrated to Minneapolis, Minnesota, and set up a successful business of grain elevators.

Thomas married Dad's grandmother, Alice Vivian Ames, in Boston on the 25th of June, 1890, the same date her parents had been married in 1863 in Cincinnati, Ohio, and the same date her daughter would be married to my grandfather in Chicago in 1919. Alice had been one of few women in history to obtain a masters degree in classics from Wellesley College and was teaching in Boston when she met Thomas. The families of both of her parents had been in America since the first Great Migration of some 20,000 English Pilgrims and Puritans who took the two-month voyage across the Atlantic between 1620, the landing of the *Mayflower*, and 1640, when the Puritans in England took control of Parliament and no longer had reason to leave.

Alice's father, Charles Gordon Ames, had been brought up by strict Congregationalist parents in Massachusetts and New Hampshire, but he was ordained a Baptist minister when he was eighteen. In 1859, after preaching around New England and Pennsylvania he switched his allegiance to become a minister in the newly formed Unitarian church, which abandoned the idea of a Trinity. In 1865, after the Civil War ended, he took a steamer around the Cape to California to found two churches. In our family archive we have the letters he wrote home to his wife in Boston describing his travels and impressions of the aftermath of the war. He returned to Boston a year later, having missed the birth of Alice's sister, Edith.

Charles was an avid supporter of the cause for women's rights and concerned about the influx of poor families from Europe at that time. Beginning in 1845 with the horrible potato famine in Ireland, millions of impoverished souls had sought refuge in America and the pace continued into the nineteenth century, creating the second Great Migration. Together with his wife Fanny, born Julia Francis Baker, Charles set up social welfare services to help them. Protestant ministers at that time became involved because the newcomers were Catholic and there was hope that these newcomers would be converted to their point of view. Fanny is listed in the *Book of Women's Firsts* by Phyllis Reed for founding the first organization of women volunteers set up to help the needy, called the Relief Society of Germantown, Pennsylvania. During the labor union discord in 1890, she also became the first female factory inspector.

Dad's paternal great-grandfather who had come to America a bit before Thomas Winter also proved the American Dream. Frederick Schroeder was fifteen when he left his home in Trier, Prussia, in 1848, arriving in Manhattan just three years after the Great Irish Migration began. Leaving a mother and brother behind, Frederick, his father and sister were fleeing political oppression, not starvation, and they came to America educated.

Barely old enough to wear long pants, Frederick started his own cigar manufacturing company, selling his wares on the sidewalk. By developing a special way of rolling tobacco, he soon had a growing business. By the time he was twenty-one he had twelve employees. A company of twenty was considered large in New York in those days. By 1870, the year his daughter Adelaide, my father's grandmother, was born, he was a partner and the president of the Germania Savings Bank and had won the office of Comptroller of New York. Five years later he was elected mayor of Brooklyn and by 1878, he was elected a state senator. Adelaide's memories of life began in a mansion in Brooklyn with a garden that filled an entire block. When I walked the Brooklyn Bridge recently, I saw Frederick's name smack in the middle of the brass plaque mounted on the face of the tower overhead which listed those who helped get it built.

The last great-grandfather was Minor Thomas Ames who married Emily Rose. Like Fanny Baker and Charles Ames, both Minor and Emily were descendants of the Pilgrims and Puritans of the first Great Migration. Just to show you how prolific and long-lived those Protestants were, when Emily's great-great-great-grandmother Abigail Rose celebrated her hundredth birthday in the Granville, Massachusetts Congregational Church in 1791, she was accompanied by her seven living children and their spouses, 110 grandchildren, over 300 great-grandchildren and some forty great-great grandchildren – in other words, over 450 living descendents. She lived to be 103.

Even though it was a tiny society and most of those Puritans intermarried, Minor Ames and Charles Ames were not related. Minor's ancestors used to spell the name *Eames*.

The first to arrive in America wearing my surname was Captain Anthony Eames. He landed at Salem with John Endecott and the New England Company (later the Massachusetts Bay Company) eight years after the *Mayflower*. One hundred eighty more of our Puritan ancestors settled in New England during the next twenty years. Today their names serve as place names around Massachusetts and Connecticut for towns, streets, buildings and rivers, such as Warren, Cushing, Mansfield, Putnam, Chaffee, Wolcott, May, Kendall, Peabody, Barker, Baker, Blodgett, Carpenter and Brewster.

Eames settled with his wife and nine children in the brand new town of Hingham, named for Hingham, England, whence its original settlers came several years before Eames. It's eleven miles below Boston on the south bay. Eames' election as captain of the town's militia started a cross-town war, for the Hingham *cluster* of families objected. They thought one of their own should have been chosen because they'd been in town longer. The result of the conflict, argued in the court of the Massachusetts Bay Colony for several years, was that Anthony moved his family out of Hingham and across the border into Marshfield in Plymouth Colony. There, his grandson and namesake Anthony married the great-grand-daughter of Richard Warren, who'd arrived on the *Mayflower*.

The next issue tackled by the Eames family was argued two generations later when, in 1690, Parliament in England decreed that the Massachusetts Bay Colony and Plymouth Colony be combined into one colony. Members of Plymouth did not practice their religion in the same way as the Puritans in the Bay Colony and therefore many, including Anthony Eames, Jr., did not want this consolidation. Rather than compromise, he moved the family to Connecticut. There his family intermarried with descendents of some of those other ancestors, one of whom had a particularly large dose of salmon blood, Thomas Knowlton.

Knowlton made such a name for himself that his life-sized bronze statue is mounted on a tall pedestal guarding the entrance to the capital building in Hartford, Connecticut, and a bronze plaque with a relief of his image adorns the wall of the economics building at Columbia University in New York. My great-grandfa-ther, grandfather and uncle would be named after him.

When he was fifteen Knowlton and one of his older twin brothers, Daniel, left their family's farm in Ashford, Connecticut to join the Rangers protecting the frontier during the French and Indian War. He was amazingly agile and skilled with a musket, leaving behind legends of dashing through bands of Indians. When the Americans succeeded, he returned to his 400-acre farm in Ashford to marry Anna Keyes and start his family. But soon his former commander, and another relative of Dad's, Israel Putnam, called Knowlton back into action. They'd learned of the Battle of Lexington and prepared to fight the British for independence.

Knowlton was immediately elected captain of his local Connecticut regiment, which was the first from a sister colony to arrive outside Boston to support the Massachusetts patriots and among the 1000 men who shortly after marched from Cambridge to fight the Battle of Bunker Hill on Breed's Hill. At the monument today is a marker on the model of the battle showing where Knowlton fought valiantly to protect the rail fence against two of General Howe's attacks, at one point having his musket shot right out of his hand. Knowlton was the last to leave the hill as he covered the backs of his retreating comrades.

His talents and courage were noted to the newly appointed General Washington when he took over the troops in Cambridge. So he employed Knowlton for several special assignments during the year-long siege of Boston, including a raid on British soldiers in Charlestown. After the British evacuated Boston, Washington prepared for a British invasion of New York and promoted Knowlton to lieutenant colonel, granting him his own regiment known as Knowlton's Rangers. Among the soldiers were Knowlton's eldest son, Frederick, and a twenty-one-year-old neighbor from Connecticut, Captain Nathan Hale.

After the Battle of Brooklyn and Washington's escape to Manhattan, he kept Knowlton's Rangers close to him and moved his headquarters into what is now called the Morris Mansion in Washington Heights (161st Street above Harlem). After the British invaded the island at Kip's Bay (23rd to 34th Streets), Washington's headquarters was cut off from the American troops in New York City at the southern tip of the island so he asked Knowlton to send one of his officers through the British ranks near Kip's Bay to gather intelligence in the city. Knowlton asked his officers for a volunteer. Captain Hale rose to the challenge. While he was gone, Knowlton stayed to protect Washington in Harlem. But when Knowlton's men met the British on the hills of Harlem Heights (site of Columbia's economics building today) he was felled by an English musket ball and died an hour later with his son at his side.

The statue of him wearing his ranger garments and carrying his sword at ready wasn't erected to commemorate his heroism until a hundred years later, along with a matching statue of Hale, carved and cast by the same artist. Hale had been captured by the British as he tried to cross back through the enemy lines just a few days after Knowlton's death. The following day Hale was tried for treason and hanged. The two statues were mounted to face each other across the expansive park by the Capitol building, but in recent years a corporation built a large building between the two of them and it is impossible to see the connection as originally intended.

Meanwhile, another of Dad's forebears was making history. He was William Dawes, called *Billy*. My grandparents kept his name in our consciousness by naming Dad's brother Bobby after him, Robert Dawes.

Billy Dawes was younger than Knowlton by five years. He grew up in Boston where his family had lived since the first William Dawes, aged fifteen, arrived on the *Planter* in 1635. Like his father and grandfather, Billy was a member of America's first regiment, the Ancient and Honorable Artillery Company, whose standard was later followed by four presidents and currently has 700 men serving in Iraq. Billy was also a member of the Sons of Liberty led and organized by Paul Revere. Billy was known for his cunning and his guile which enabled him during the war to cross through enemy lines more successfully than Hale had. One of Billy's first acts of patriotism before the war even started was to steal two large cannon from under the noses of the British and hide them away to be used by the patriots.

The event by which Billy was most noted – as is still reenacted yearly in Boston – was his participation as an express rider on the ht of April 18, 1775. Since Billy was an excellent horseman, aul Revere had chosen him to be one of thirty special riders to be on the alert that night to ride into the countryside and spread the news when the British marched from Boston to Lexington and Concord. The director of the Sons of Liberty, Joseph Warren (another cousin), dispatched Billy on his ride thirty minutes before Revere, who'd been busy at the North Church. However, Billy traveled the longer land route and rode a slower horse and thus arrived in Lexington a half hour after Revere.

The two men then rode together with a third rider, Samuel Prescott, towards Concord. But no sooner had they left the edge of town in Lexington, than an ambush of British regulars snared and forced them into a fenced pen.

Prescott was the only one to escape successfully and spread the news to Concord. Though Billy was also able to flee the holding pen, he was soon thrown from his horse. The horse dashed into the darkness, leaving Billy to walk back to Lexington. Revere had remained captive by the British for questioning. He was soon released, but since the British had taken his mighty steed for themselves, he also walked back to Lexington. Both men probably witnessed the "shot heard round the world" that began the revolution.

Billy fought at the Battle of Bunker Hill along with Knowlton, but was probably with the regiment from Boston guarding the redoubt on the other side of the battleground.

William Dawes is remembered by a monument in the form of brass horseshoes embedded in the sidewalk on the Cambridge Commons indicating where he galloped through town on that fateful night. A bronze plaque mounted on the wall between a MacDonalds and a Dunkin' Donuts across the street from Boston's Feneuil Hall marks where once stood his birthplace.

None of the Eames men in Dad's line were soldiers in the Revolutionary War. Abner, the fifth generation, was forty-four when America declared independence, and his son Joel was only twelve. Abner was involved in a squabble of his own in his hometown, this one over taxes, a cause which was close to my father's heart. The problem was a common one in those days and led to the eventual division of church and state. In the first colonial New England towns, tax money paid for the minister's living and for building the town's church. That was fine when there was only one parish, the Congregational church. Now there were many different churches, including Baptist, Methodist, Jewish and Quaker. To accommodate them, compromises were made in the Congregationalist church membership rules which Abner considered a travesty. He wanted things to stay as they had been traditionally, and when that didn't happen he did what his forebears had done. He left town.

Hoping a new life in the frontier would allow him to run his life the way he wanted to, or at least get him out of the way of pillaging British, Hessian and American soldiers, Abner packed his family of nine children onto wagons and mules and headed to the wildest and westernmost settlement in Massachusetts. He and his brother purchased a farm in Becket in the Housatonic Valley of the Berkshire Hills. The only access to the town was over the very steep grade Henry Knox had just conquered dragging the artillery he'd captured from Ticonderoga – the road usually couldn't be traveled in winter. The Eames family stayed in Becket for the next hundred years and three generations.

It wasn't unusual to change the spelling of names in those days. There was no standardized spelling in the English language until the *Oxford English Dictionary* was completed in 1928. When Abner died in 1812, his son Joel, who thought the "E" at the beginning of our name was superfluous, changed the spelling to Ames. Joel married Azubah Putnam, a cousin thrice removed of Thomas Knowlton's commander, General Israel Putnam. Joel's and Azubah's third child Justin married Anna Harriet Chaffee, Thomas Knowlton's granddaughter. They had ten children, five daughters and five sons, and christened their seventh Thomas Miner Ames. Thomas Miner modified his name also and by the time he was a grown man was known as Minor Thomas, remembered by those who succeeded him as the man who began building the family fortune.

My great grandfather, Knowlton Lyman Ames

CHAPTER SIXTEEN

Building the Empire

My father used to call his great-grandfather *Minor-T*. Born on the Becket family farm in 1839, Minor-T grew up during the height of the industrial boom when the railway was a major part of life – Becket's link to east and west – and watched both his grandfathers make their living off the Boston & Albany line. The huge woodpile at the Becket train station needed continuous replenishing to feed the hungry steam engines chugging over the steep grade. Justin Ames harvested trees for lumber and Minor's mother's family, the Thomas Chaffees, burned the wood to make a grade of charcoal so fine it was shipped to ironwork factories as far away as India.

At seventeen Minor-T was ready to "Go West, Young Man." In 1855 he left his eight siblings and his family's successful business with "only the change in his pocket, and a good head on his shoulders" plus his love and understanding of the railroad business.

He worked for two railroads, making his way through upstate New York to Columbus, Ohio, where he became acquainted with a successful rope manufacturer Lyman Rose and his wife Jane, neé Dawes, William Dawes' granddaughter. Their daughter Emily caught Minor-T's attention. However, just before the Civil War broke out, Emily consented to marry a friend of her brother's, a Mr. French. When the South seceded, her brother and Mr. French left to fight for the Union. Even though Minor-T was opposed to slavery, it appears he did not put on a uniform, which would still have been a voluntary choice in Ohio.

One night while standing under a tree waiting for a storm to pass, Emily's brother and Mr. French were struck by lightening and killed, leaving Emily a widow. Minor-T saw his opening and asked her to marry him.

In September of the following year, with the Civil War still raging, Minor-T moved to Chicago. By now twenty-three, he was once again a stranger in a new town with nothing except his love of Emily, his bride of five months. Soon he got a job as a salesman for a coal company and quickly prospered, building a comfortable home for the family.

Industrialists were figuring out it was cheaper to fuel trains with coal than with the wood grown by Minor-T's father. Some, including Minor-T, suspected that pockets of America's black gold lay underneath the fertile prairies to the west, right where they were needed to fuel the trains passing overhead.

In 1864, a small group of investors, friends of Minor-T, began searching for coal near a tiny town called Minonk, 120 miles southwest of Chicago in the middle of the corn fields. They discovered a high-grade vein almost three feet wide at a depth of 553 feet, but their money began running out. When they asked Minor-T to be a partner, he consented, eventually becoming the company president.

Many factors contributed to Minor-T's success. There still was no such thing as income tax. Coal fueled all the machines produced by the Industrial Revolution, including the steamships taking New Englanders like Charles Gordon Ames around the Cape to California and furnaces for homes. Labor was cheap and plentiful because this was the time of the second Great Migration. The company placed ads on the East Coast to entice workers from Poland, Russia and Germany to come west with promising wages. Soon 400 men were working the shafts extracting 500 tons of coal daily from two mines on one seam. The town grew to 3000.

Emily gave birth to their first child (my dad's grandfather, Knowlton Lyman Ames, the future Mystery Man) in 1868. By that time the family had moved to Minonk where the Coal and Tile Company, which was also the largest producer of drainage tile in the world, was the principal source of income for the town. Two sisters, Jane and Harriet, followed. But when Knowlton was nine, Jane seven and Harriet five, their mother died. She was thirty-six.

Since Minor-T couldn't keep up with the business and care for his children, he sent them back to Columbus to live with their grandfather, Lyman Rose. Minor-T then married Irene Cowan, sister to his brother's wife, but they had no children and he never sent for his own to repair his broken family.

Minor-T was succumbing to kidney disease (known then as Bright's disease), which would eventually kill him thirteen years later. Midwestern Americans already had poor diets with too few fresh vegetables and too much starch and fat, causing many digestive problems. Doctors were scarce in the West and medicines were mostly ineffective in those days. Those that appeared to give results, due to the high percentage of alcohol and opium in their ingredients, were taken in large quantities. These probably made Minor-T's condition even worse and he became the first Eames/Ames male since coming to America to die before reaching age seventy. Sadly, Minor-T's son, grandson and great-grandson wouldn't fare much better than he did.

As Chicago rebuilt herself after the fire of 1871, there was hope she would be the site for the upcoming exposition planned to celebrate the 400-year anniversary of Columbus' discovery of America. A whole building would be dedicated to mining. Minor-T was part of the leadership creating the new technology to be shown off at the exposition. One of his friends, Thomas A. Edison, had just completed building two electric generators and was trying to sell the idea of incandescent lighting. Minor-T enlisted Edison to help solve the problem of lighting the shafts of his mines and in 1882 brought him to Minonk.

Instead of each miner lightening his own way with a dangerous and cumbersome carbide lamp attached to his cap, Edison figured he could string a line of incandescent lamps through the shafts to light the passageway. He called for one of his generators, placed it near the mine and strung the wires. The plan worked so perfectly Minor-T and Edison decided to string a wire down the middle of Minonk's main thoroughfare. Today, the little town of Minonk, which shrank back to 2000 residents at the end of the coal era, claims to be the first town to have had incandescent street lighting. That same year Edison lit Pearl Street in New York City and eventually 93,000 incandescent lights would illuminate the Columbian Exposition as electricity began zapping away the uses for coal. But Minor-T would not be alive to see it.

———◆———

My great-grandfather Knowlton was probably better off not breathing the polluted air of Chicago as he grew up. Leaving Ohio at thirteen, he boarded a train bound for New Jersey to join the rest of the third-form students at the Lawrenceville School to prepare for college. Knowlton was like his namesake in many ways. Tall, and more agile than strong, he used his inherited desire to challenge barriers by becoming a football player. Within a short time at Lawrenceville, he was being called *Snake* for the way he slithered through the opposition to the goal line. The name stuck. After Lawrenceville, he attended Princeton where by the end of his junior year, he was making football history, being credited with the invention of the drop kick. His Princeton records were kept for a hundred years when, *post mortem*, he was inducted into the College Football Hall of Fame in South Bend, Indiana.

At the Princeton senior prom, Snake met Adelaide Schroeder, the beautiful and pampered daughter of Frederick Schroeder, who by that time was a New York state senator. "Though Snake had reached the height of his fame, and supposedly swept Adelaide off her feet with an ardent courtship, she refused him three times before she consented to marry him," wrote their daughter Rosemary in her manuscript on our family. Snake probably had no idea he was the first Eames/Ames in 270 years to marry someone outside the English Puritan gene pool emanating from the first Great Migration. Only now was America becoming a *melting pot*.

The 1870s had been big years for America's industrialists. By 1880 a mere 4,047 men held most of America's wealth and among that number were Minor-T Ames and Frederick Schroeder. But, in 1890, just as Snake was achieving his football fame, finishing college and proposing to Adelaide, Minor-T died. He was buried with his wife and the rest of Chicago's wealthy in the Graceland Cemetery.

The management of the coal and tile company was soon transferred to twenty-two-year-old Snake. Society-loving Adelaide, who was twenty at their wedding, was not at all happy when they left New York shortly after to set up housekeeping in tiny Minonk. The marriage was soon in trouble and the coal mine was close behind.

While the empires of the rich few had been growing larger and larger, the gap between the owners and the workers had been widening alarmingly. Everyone was grabbing for the same dollar bill. Finally the bottom fell out. In 1893, in spite of the hoopla at the Columbian Exposition in Chicago, America sank into a deep recession. Banks closed, businesses failed and people were out of work. The price of coal took a nosedive.

The Minonk Coal and Tile Company had its share of union discord. During one strike when Snake and the coal miners were fighting over the last pieces of the pie, two men were accidentally killed. One was a young miner, the other Snake's manager. Things went from bad to worse until finally Snake allowed the company to go into foreclosure.

Fortunately for the Ames family, when the profits of the mine had been good, Snake had made other investments and built a corporation with many subsidiary companies called Booth Fisheries. Once he was rid of the mine, he moved his family to Evanston, Illinois, a wealthy suburb fourteen miles from Chicago. There he concentrated on Booth Fisheries and was back on the road to becoming one of the most influential businessmen in the Midwest.

My grandfather, Knowlton Lyman Ames, Jr., was born ten months after Snake and Adelaide were married. His nickname in those days was *Juny*. Soon he had a tiny sister named Alys, but she died when she was five of diphtheria. Her death devastated Snake more than the loss of his mine. Several years later my father's Uncle John was born and finally his redheaded aunt, Rosemary, the family genealogist and chronologist.

Juny followed his father's footsteps to Lawrenceville and

Princeton, playing football and even adopting his father's nickname Snake. A recent program from a Princeton game stated in a "Memories" column he scored the first touchdown in the Palmer Memorial Stadium when the Tigers defeated Dartmouth, sixteen to twelve on October 2, 1915.

Though similar in talent and competitive drive, Dad's grandfather Snake and father Juny appear to have been motivated by different things. Snake pushed himself for achievement, taking his glory from a job well done, whereas Juny went after power and social position. "Juny grew up in a family that worshipped the almighty dollar," wrote his sister Rosemary. "His cronies were the jet-setters of their day, the personalities whose activities made the gossip columns. And, sad to say, usually the heavy drinkers. Juny sought color and life, and people always moving in high gear. He was magnetic, with a quick, creative mind and a marvelous ability to make droll comments. Every time I introduced him to a woman friend, they promptly fell for him. The broken nose caused by a football injury only seemed to increase his charm. When we went to the theatre in New York, he would know at least a half-dozen people in the audience who all seemed very glad to see him."

Dad's father met the first of his four wives while serving his country in France during World War I as an army lieutenant. This was Dad's mother, Edith Ames Winter from Minneapolis, who'd been volunteering for the American Fund for French Wounded there. She was described as a tall, stunning woman with bobbed brown hair and eyes as blue as Juny's were. Edith and Juny met at a club in Paris and it's easy to imagine how sparks ignited. Since Edith's middle name was Ames, the surname of her maternal grandparents, Juny's last name must have caught her attention.

Their marriage was announced in the *Minneapolis Journal's* social pages with a photo the width of the entire page showing their wedding party with ten attendants on each side. The headline blazoned, "Edith Ames Winter Is Wed to Knowlton Ames; Hundreds at Ceremony. Marriage Is Culmination of Romance Begun When Both Were in Service Overseas – Couple Will Go on Extended Wedding Trip, Including Ocean Voyage."

Their home would be Chicago, which would be a big change for Edith.

Chicago in the 1920s

CHAPTER SEVENTEEN

Growing Up in Chicago

"Our mother just couldn't fit into the rough and tumble life of Chicago when she married our father," Dad's older brother Bud told me. I went to see him a few years ago in Chicago where he'd lived all his life. He had just celebrated his eightieth birthday and was suffering from emphysema after smoking since he was a teenager. He lived in a tiny apartment, the rent for which he borrowed from his daughter, so we met in a McDonald's near the center of town. Dressed in a well-worn suit and tie, he greeted me with my father's grin. I hadn't seen him since our visit with his family on our way home from Italy when I was eight, forty-one years earlier. I wanted him to show me where the family had lived, played and worked when Dad was born and he eagerly obliged.

We left his car at McDonald's and drove my rental up Michigan Avenue to the middle of the fashionable shopping district. Our first stop was the elegant Drake Hotel. Like Dad, he talked nonstop. "After the war, it was easy for our father to step back into his set of society friends. He grew up here. But our mother's friends were still in Minneapolis, where her parents were. Her Wellesley classmates were mostly on the East Coast."

Bud motioned for me to walk in front of him through the large mahogany revolving door into the hotel. Ahead of us was a grand staircase leading up to an expansive lobby on the second floor. Halfway up he said, "Stop here. I want to tell you a story that took place on these stairs.

"One of Mother's best college friends was named Margaret and she lived in New York City. Mom wanted her to visit and wrote Margaret telling her life here with our dad was just one party after another, begging Margaret to come stay for a few weeks, claiming the museums were lovely and that we had fabulous new department stores here on Michigan Avenue. That kind of thing.

"'Impossible,' Margaret wrote back. 'I read the papers. They say Al Capone is shooting people dead on the streets of Chicago. I'm not going to take a chance.'

"Nonetheless, after several months of persuading, and reminding her that Capone started his career in New York City, Mom convinced Margaret to make the trip. She would stay at the Drake here, right by the shopping district.

"Margaret arrived in Chicago in the early hours of the morning on the Twentieth Century Limited and caught a Yellow Cab which deposited her right there at the entrance to the hotel, which she entered through those revolving doors. No sooner had she ascended halfway up this staircase than a gangster dashed through those same revolving doors right behind her with a gun in his hands. After several deafening gunshots, another man, who'd been standing right here next to Margaret, became a spouting fountain of blood and bits of flesh and collapsed dead right about here on the same stair where she was about to place her next step.

"Instantly, Margaret did an about-face, grabbing the arm of the bellboy who was carrying her massive luggage. She fled down this staircase, back through those revolving doors and threw herself and her bulky mink coat into another cab sitting at the curb. 'The railroad station,' she shouted to the cabby and then ended up sitting on a bench there the rest of the day waiting for the next train to New York City. Needless to say, she never came back to Chicago again."

My dad had told me that their mother's family, the Winters, were quite different from their father's family. Since their mother was also descended from Richard Warren of the *Mayflower*, my grandparents were ninth cousins. My grandmother's family had managed to retain the religious values and traditions brought by the Pilgrims, but Minor-T had left these behind in Massachusetts when he forged West.

"Our mother's parents were active church members," said Bud. "While Grandfather Winter ran his grain elevator business in Minneapolis he volunteered for civic affairs, helping set up the park system there. Our grandmother had followed her mother Fanny Baker's footsteps and had become the queen of do-gooders. She was the president of a national women's volunteer organization called the Federation of Women and in the family archives we have thank-you letters signed by Herbert Hoover for the good things she did as well as an invitation to the White House from President Harding!"

My grandmother Edith's experience of women's rights was probably affirmed when she followed her mother's path to Wellesley. It's possible she had little idea how chauvinistic men could be on occasion until she was the wife and daughter-in-law of football stars.

After visiting the Drake Hotel, Uncle Bud and I drove to the north end of State Parkway which would have been a nice walk north towards Lincoln Park when Bud was younger. This is still a beautiful, tree-lined avenue of elegantly kept brownstones. We parked in front of an attractive apartment house two doors up from the Ambassador Hotel.

"Our family flat occupied a full story on the second floor," Bud said as he pulled a creased city map out of his coat's inside pocket. With a nicotine-stained finger, he indicated the spot on the map where we were standing. "This area was the Gold Coast, Money Town. That's North State Parkway, Money Street. Over here is Astor Street, also Money Street. Over here is Less Money Street," he said pointing two streets west of State. "But here," he said, tracing the road east along Lake Michigan, "is Lake Shore Drive. Money, money, money. That's where your great-grandfather Snake lived.

"Our grandmother Nanna Adelaide had divorced him by then because he was messing around with a woman named Ada. Nanna Adelaide moved back to New York and bought a huge Victorian house near Grandfather Schroeder's summer home on Shelter Island off Long Island. Then Snake shacked up with Ada. She became our step-grandmother and they had a baby who was younger than I, my baby half-aunt, Emily." (She was named after Snake's mother, Emily Rose.)

"Did you see much of your real grandmother Nanna after that?" I asked.

"Sure. From then on, at the beginning of each winter, she took the Twentieth Century Limited from New York to Chicago to stay a few weeks at the Ambassador and visit us. She always ate at one of the tables by the window of the front room. It used to be called the Oak Room and looked out on the street. Your dad and I passed the Ambassador several times a day coming and going to school and she'd wave to us. There were two colored doormen there named Willy and Bob. Wonderful men. They always waved hello to us, too.

"Then after seeing us, she continued west on the Sante Fe train to Pasadena where she spent the rest of her winter in the warmth and luxury of the Huntington Hotel. They had black-tie dinners, tennis and swimming, even though it was winter, and famous Hollywood guests hanging around. When the winter season ended, Nanna did the same thing in reverse.

"The Ambassador Hotel was a center of high society in those days. That's where all the celebrities hung out and they all knew Willy and Bob. They could get booze there during Prohibition any time they wanted. The bartenders were always mixing up newly famous concoctions.

"Chicago for our parents in the 1920s was party-party, spend-spend, party-party. One night a famous chanteuse named Helen Morgan came to the apartment to sing. During a break, she came into the bedroom your dad and I were sharing and sang us a lullaby.

"Prohibition was on and Chicago was the speakeasy town. Booze was flowing and it went right into our home. The elevator opened directly into the lobby of our apartment. One morning I answered the door to find an old colored man standing there with a heavy bundle hanging from each arm. 'Tell yo' Mama I got da stuff,' he said. Two five-gallon tins of pure bathtub gin! Made right over on the West Side of Chicago!"

Between 1925 and 1930 Capone reportedly made 100 million dollars a year with his breweries, distilleries, speakeasies, bookie joints, gambling houses, brothels, race tracks and nightclubs. The Ames family didn't have near that much, but nonetheless Bud said, "Your dad was born with a silver spoon in his mouth. If there was anyone with money, we had it."

Dad's mother Edith traveled the 354 miles northwest to her parents' house in Minneapolis for the last month of each pregnancy. Uncle Bud, christened Knowlton Lyman Ames III, was born in 1920, Dad followed in 1922 and Uncle Bobby completed the trio in 1925 – the same year my mother was born in London.

Bud continued. "As children on State Parkway, a normal day for us started early when our nanny Mrs. Carpenter or *Cook* woke us up. Our Pop was usually long gone, having left for work or to go play golf. Our mother was still in her bedroom, usually incommunicado, recovering from the previous evening. We don't remember when Mom began to drink too much. We just remember that she did.

"We boys dressed ourselves, always in shorts, even in Chicago's coldest weather. Your dad and I wore jackets and ties to school, but little Bobby just wore tee shirts. He had a favorite pair of gray flannel shorts that he wore every day until they were entirely worn out. Mother finally threw them into the fireplace one night to stop him from wearing them.

"Cook fed us breakfast in the kitchen. While we ate we often watched her fix a breakfast tray for our mother. There would be a starched, white lace doily with a flower in a Japanese lacquer vase. All Mom ever ate was dry toast and black coffee, but the tray also had her cigarette lighter and a matching crystal cup with a bouquet of cigarette filters sticking out from its rim. That was for dessert.

"Our dad was busy climbing the career staircase, with a great deal of help from our grandfather, Snake. His first position after he married our mother was advertising manager of American Steel Foundries, a subsidiary of Booth Fisheries. When Snake founded the *Chicago Journal of Commerce*, another subsidiary, he put Dad in charge. But our old man did a lousy job running his father's paper.

His interests leaned more towards playing golf, fishing, partying and chasing women. Hence, in 1927 when I was seven and your dad was five, Snake pushed our father aside and replaced him with his younger brother, Uncle John.

"This really angered our father, but he regrouped quickly. He appealed to his good friend John Hertz for a job. A few years earlier, Hertz had founded The Yellow Cab Company. Starting with a small stake in a car dealership, Hertz quickly made it into a profitable business. He'd taken the yellow and black color scheme for his cabs from Chicago's horse-drawn trolleys and used it again when he started his well known rental-car company.

"Hertz made our father president of the company of which he was chairman, but our old man stayed only one year. He still held a grudge against his brother and father for booting him out of the *Journal*. So when he learned that William Hearst had put the *Chicago Evening Post* on the market, he saw an opportunity to get even and bought it, establishing himself as a full-fledged competitor to the *Journal*.

He was hoping to ruin the *Journal* altogether. When our Grandfather Snake went on a business trip to Europe, Dad approached his brother John and tried to convince him to use the *Post* for all of the *Journal's* typesetting. This would have put the control of both papers in our father's hands. Uncle John got wise to the scheme and notified their father (Snake) who came home from Europe on the next boat in a huff, just in time to stop the plan. But the rift between the brothers was never mended."

Uncle Bud and I took a walk around the neighborhood. It was far more luxurious than mine had been, growing up in Sierra Madre. Lincoln Park, an elegant playground bordering shining Lake Michigan, was three blocks north on State Parkway.

"When we were little," Bud said, "Mrs. Carpenter escorted us here to see the animals in the zoo. When we were old enough to walk to the park by ourselves, we liked to go to that small pond over there and row around in rented boats."

He and I walked around the block to see The Latin School, which he and Dad attended, and the Episcopal church where their mother occasionally took them when she woke up early enough. "That's about the only place where we heard the word God used in a reverent manner," Bud said.

Even though Snake and Juny had been star football players in college, neither of them attempted to teach the game or throw a ball with the boys. It wasn't a neighborhood that invited street games. However, Bud pointed out the Racquet Club two blocks south of the apartment. "It was an all-men's club at that time and you had to sit next to Jesus Christ to belong. We swam nude in the pool there on Saturdays and our Uncle John was president of the board."

"Did you have things like Little League baseball or play in intramural sports?" I asked.

"No, we never played in any organized sports. We roller-skated and that kind of thing, but as we got older, we concocted our own brand of street action. One day, in fact it was Halloween, we were hanging around Burton Parkway, which crosses North State Parkway back by the apartment. It's a great crossing for taxicabs going back and forth between Lake Shore Drive and the Ambassador. Your dad and I and some of our friends stood, three on each side of the road, like this," he said, putting his body in the hunched position of someone playing tug-of-war. "One in back of the other holding onto an imaginary rope out in front of us.

"These taxi drivers would come down Burton Street and out of the corner of their eyes they could see boys theoretically holding a rope across the road. The taxi drivers would slam on their brakes.

They'd get out, and say, 'Ah! I can see what you kids are doing,' and then they'd look all around for the rope. There was nothing. We'd just stand there with nothing.

"Another favorite pastime of ours was pouring rice into car radiators, but forget I told you that. What your dad liked to do most of all was visit the two little girls who lived down the street, Diana and Molly Hill. I think they were a little younger than he. He preferred their company far more to ours. We couldn't get him out of the place. He just loved sitting around their kitchen table telling stories."

As Bud was telling me this, I thought of my own son, who at five liked to go across the street where two girls his age lived, and while the family ate dinner, sit with them making jokes or telling stories about his day, just to make them laugh.

"We were surrounded by important people doing fascinating things." Bud said. "One friend of our parents was Commander E.F. McDonald Jr., known as *Gene*. His story is kind of like the story of those guys in Silicon Valley who started a computer business in their garage. Several years earlier, in 1918, Gene and another wireless-radio enthusiast set up a factory on their kitchen table in Chicago to make radio equipment for other amateurs. By 1923, Zenith Radio Corporation was launched. They took their trademark from the founders' amateur radio station, 9ZN and sold the first radios under Z-Nith.

"Anyway, Gene owned a yacht christened the *Mizpah*. One warm summer weekend he invited our family to spend the afternoon cruising Lake Michigan. Your dad and I got to watch the adults skeet shooting off the back of the upper deck.

"Lots of these people bought vacation places to get away from Chicago's biting cold winter weather, so in 1926 the old man had bought a large home on 40 George Street in Nassau in the Bahamas and began spending several months each winter there. It was a haven for two of his passions, drinking and fishing, and probably a third. Our mother took us to join him during our school vacations.

"It was a three-day trip from Chicago to Nassau. We departed at night on the Twentieth Century Limited and slept in luxury overnight compartments as the train carried us to Grand Central Terminal in New York City. Then we boarded the *Munargo*, an odd-looking ship, part cruise ship and part freighter. The trip from New York ended two days later when we pulled into the harbor at Nassau. On the ocean side, in those days, was an island called Hog Island. Today it's called Paradise Island and there's now a bridge, but then you had to cross the channel on little shuttles. A club there called the Porcupine Club had beautiful, untrampled beaches. It was a money club. We were members there.

"Remember, this was during Prohibition, but Nassau was a British Colony so we had a full bar, supposedly the longest bar in the islands, on the second floor of 40 George Street for doing the kind of entertaining our old man did. He had this ChrisCraft motorboat. The driver's name was Rollins, a black man. Often, while we were out on that boat, another boat passed by with a guy on deck with a machine gun. We just knew to look away. Those boys were rumrunners, taking booze from Cuba through Nassau to Florida and the old man knew all of them. There was a place called Dirty Dick's where everyone hung out."

Uncle Bud and I finished our circle of his old neighborhood, stopping at number 1530 North State Parkway, which was an even nicer apartment house than 1330. "Our father did well in business and when your dad was seven and I was nine, he moved us up the street to this building. It had just been built and we were the first tenants to move in. Once again our apartment took up an entire floor. We moved just before the stock-market crash, but of course we didn't know it was coming."

Bud had a really proud look on his face when I took his photo in front of the polished brass entry. The building today is still one of the most elegant in town. We were a stone's throw from Lincoln Park and directly across the street from a mansion that stood in the middle of a block covered with grass and shady trees, until recently the home of the Roman Catholic archbishop for Chicago.

"By that time our parents were not getting along at all well," said Bud. "They had separate bedrooms and Mom was drinking more than ever. There were terrible yelling matches when both of them were drunk. Mom stopped taking us to join our father in Nassau. The old man, on the other hand, went there more and more frequently. Bit by bit, his money traveled there, too."

In March of 1929, the first panic hit the stock market but people like Charles Mitchell bailed it out. Snake went on a business trip to Europe, thinking he was safe. In September, stocks began to collapse again. Snake and his friends still remained positive. On October 24 the free fall began. The ocean liner that took Snake home wasn't one of the only two ships with facilities for stock trading. By the time he reached home, October 29 was history, and his overly leveraged business empire was in ruins.

Much to his credit, while most people sold out, Snake didn't, taking a lot of the losses himself. When the money was counted, he was in debt against Booth Fisheries and personal investments to the tune of six million dollars, mainly to banks. In today's figures that would be about sixty-five million. The losses from the crash overwhelmed Snake. All his friends were in the same boat. He had nowhere to go and no one to turn to. His estate was valued at a mere $50,000. However, exactly a year earlier, he'd established a life insurance trust of 1.1 million dollars.

"Mr. Ames recently suffered a nervous breakdown and for a week remained away from his office in the Booth Fisheries Company," said one newspaper clipping. Everyone was worried about Snake, and his chauffeur was given strict orders not to leave him alone. On December 23, 1931, the very date the life insurance policy payment was due, Snake asked the chauffeur to stop the limousine in front of a drug store, complaining of a headache. They were across from Lincoln Park and around the corner from Dad's family's apartment.

Snake asked the chauffeur to go into the store and buy some medicine. While he was gone, Snake pulled out a revolver he had hidden in a side pocket of the car and shot himself in the head. The news covered the front page of every major newspaper on the East Coast and Midwest. More than thirteen banks filed claims for their pieces of the six million dollars against Booth Fisheries. Since there was no money to be had, the banks went after Snake's estate and life insurance claim, but a Judge Taylor ruled the trust to be inviolate. It is because of the prevalence of such suicides during this era in history that suicide became a bar to collecting on such policies.

The insurance money went mostly to Uncle John to keep the paper, to Snake's widow Ada and her baby Emily, who was five when her father killed himself. Juny and his sister Rosemary, who'd alienated herself from her father by going to Hollywood to become an actress against his wishes, received nothing.

My dad was nine years old. I have heard this story told over and over by every member of the Ames family for as long as I can remember and my aunts and uncles still keep talking about it. For them it was a date as important as December 7, 1941, and a memory as big as September 11, 2001, will always be for me. They lost many things: a beloved grandfather, most of their money and all of their social prestige.

"The family was so divided by this time that at Snake's funeral the warring factions sat in separate corners," Bud said. By now we were back at the McDonald's where Bud's car was still parked and were finishing our conversation over styrofoam cups of tea. "I was given the charge of taking care of Nanna. She and I sat in one corner while Ada and baby Emily were in another. Mother and the old man were fighting each other, so they sat in separate corners. Uncle John was pitted against the old man, so they had to be separated. I don't even remember if Rosemary was there."

"What did your dad do if he didn't get any money?" I asked

"Oh, he'd made his own money and while other people were jumping off buildings, including the one next door to our new apartment, he was out having a good time. He had a mistress, too, named Frances. He would take your dad and me to her place with him and introduce her to us as Aunt Frances. Mom was still around. It was awful.

"Just to show you what kind of guy he was, in the dining room he kept a large fish tank about four feet long and eighteen inches high. It was compartmentalized with six moveable dividers. In each compartment he kept a Siamese fighting fish who would nose up to the divider just aching to get at the fish in the next compartment. Sometimes, just for the pleasure of it, my dad would take out one of the dividers and watch while two fish fought each other to the death.

"He started doing nasty things to make life difficult for our mother. In one act of spite, he yanked your dad and me out of the Latin School which was only a half-block away from our new house and sent us a mile down the road to the public Ogden School. He made us walk that mile rain, snow or shine!" Bud said with bitterness in his voice, remembering this event of nearly seventy years earlier. "Here was my millionaire father making us walk in Chicago's blistering cold weather, not even footing up the fare for a bus ticket!

"A year later, our mother had had enough. By that time her parents, Grandpa and Grandma Winter, had retired to Pasadena. When her father's health had begun to falter a few years earlier, they'd moved from Minneapolis to enjoy California's warm, dry climate. When our mother told them how unhappy she was they invited her to bring us out there and stay for a while in a little cottage at the back of their property.

"Our mother did much more than visit. It was too hard to get a divorce in Chicago in those days, but in Nevada you could get a legal divorce if you'd been living there for six weeks. There were ranches set up in Reno where the train went through. Women who could afford it stayed at the ranches while they waited. Claire Booth Luce featured one of those ranches in her play *The Women*. Did you see the movie of it?

"That's what our mother did. She left on a train for Reno, stayed the required six weeks, obtained her "quickie" divorce from our old man and continued straight on to California. Then she called for your dad and Bobby and never returned to Chicago again.

"Why didn't she call for you?"

"At the time I asked her to let me stay in the custody of our father, a decision I immediately regretted, for the first thing he did was ship me off to the Shattuck Military Academy. I was thirteen. Your dad was eleven and Bobby was eight when, unchaperoned, they boarded the Sante Fe train bound for California and our mother. I didn't see my mother or brothers again for four years. And our father didn't see them, either.

"What happened to the Mystery Man while you were away at school?"

Bud laughed. He knew that was my dad's nickname for their father. "He was as busy as ever with his business and financial activities. In 1936 he became the director of finance for the state of Illinois under Governor Henry Horner and wrote a book about it called *The A-B-C of Illinois State Finance*. I'll send you a copy.

"He also wanted to get back to the business of wooing his mistress Frances. She was really a witch! Our butler didn't like her much, either. He thought she was such an unpleasant woman that one night he put my pet snake in her bed. By the time I saw your father again, our old man had divorced her and moved permanently out of the country to his home in Nassau. That way he didn't have to pay alimony to either of his ex-wives."

Dad's Aunt Rosemary, third from left, with the rest of the cast for the movie "Our Little Girl" in 1935

CHAPTER EIGHTEEN

Pasadena in the 1930s

Los Angeles County in 1933 had an enormously diverse population. Wealthy white people in Pasadena owned expensive hotels like the Huntington where Nanna Adelaide stayed, which imported poor black people from the South to serve them. A powerful Klu Klux Klan influenced the police department in Long Beach, which tried to squelch dock workers' strikes by throwing their socialist supporters, like my Grandfather Hopkins and his friend Upton Sinclair, into jail when they read the *Bill of Rights* at a union meeting.

There was my religiously conservative great-grandmother, Alice Winter, who lived in Pasadena but worked in Hollywood as the director of the public and studio service department of the Motion Picture Producers and Distributors of America, Inc., often called the Will Hayes organization for short. It enacted the Hayes Code in 1930 to uphold the "sanctity of the institution of marriage and the home" and pledging that "No picture shall be produced that will lower the moral standards of those who see it." My Great-grandmother Winter was passionately opposed to moviemakers reaping a profit from screening movies with pornography.

My father's move to California required that he adjust to the difference between the materialistic ethics of his father's family and the puritanical ethics of his mother's. In Chicago, he'd been part of a renowned family where the priority was to have connections, money and roots. In California where everyone was a transplant, many were trying to make something out of nothing so the emphasis was on being smart, capable, or at least entertaining. Eleven-year-old Tommy Ames was no longer looking up at big business tycoons, but at Hollywood moguls.

My Grandmother Edith was thirty-three when she divorced and became a single mother of three. That's the same age I was when I divorced and became a single mother of two. My résumé included a teacher's credential and five years' experience, whereas hers would have said: "Chicago socialite, 1920-1933. Skills: Ability to sort a bridge hand in less than five seconds and an understanding of all the nuances of high society."

When I went out on my own for the second time in my life, I had alimony, child support, joint custody and ownership of the cottage where my children were living. When my grandmother fled from my grandfather, there was nothing in the cookie jar, so she and two of her three sons moved in with her parents. Her father, despite his weak health, was enjoying his retirement. On the other hand, her mother, Alice, who'd been a volunteer in Minneapolis, had written a book about volunteering (*The Business of Being a Club Woman*) and gone on tour across the country speaking over 3,000 times about volunteerism. Now, at age sixty-four in California, she was holding her first paid position. My father soon discovered there would be no apple pies in his grandmother's oven.

As director of the Hayes Organization, our dad's Grandmother Winter helped the commission keep sex and violence out of movies. These *sinful* activities had sold seats during the roaring '20s when elegant theaters had been built to accommodate them. The Depression soon sobered the overly leveraged movie industry just as it did my great-grandfather, Snake. Spotting this window of opportunity to wage war against the *devil*, religious groups throughout the nation stepped in to fix *Sin City*, their name for Hollywood, and the now-penniless *sinners* were helpless to stop them.

In 1933 Catholic bishops throughout the country gathered to establish the Legion of Decency, which strengthened the role of the Hayes Organization and nearly boycotted films altogether. Mae West lost her contract for commenting to Cary Grant, "Why don't you come up and see me sometime?" A kiss on the silver screen could last only one and a half seconds. At one point, even farm scenes showing the milking of cows were banned. Any movie shown in a public theater during the 1930s without a seal of approval from the Motion Picture Producers and Distributors of America was slapped with a fine of twenty-five grand.

Alice was perfect for this job. Her community work had introduced her to influential people throughout the country interested in raising America's moral standards. Besides Hoover and President Harding, her friends included Madame Curie and Walt Disney. And then there was her church. Alice had been brought up to follow the Puritan ethic.

"I remember your great-grandparents well," said Priscilla Morman, whom I met when visiting my mother in Pasadena a few years ago. "She and my parents were best friends. They were all teetotalers and active members of the Pasadena Presbyterian Church."

Something about this picture of my great-grandparents didn't jibe with what I knew of their daughter who had moved in with them. Wasn't alcohol the stuff their daughter couldn't live without?

My grandmother's divorce, the first in her family, came at a time when divorce was rare. My divorce, on the other hand, was merely the first one in my set of friends. Common as divorce had bcome, I was surprised to find that while some of my friends understood and were supportive, others mounted moralistic campaigns to make me change my mind.

My dentist, for example, thought it was his job to scold me, while he had my mouth clamped open so he could replace a crown I'd cracked while gritting my teeth during the night. "I hear you are getting a divorce?" he asked, knowing I couldn't answer him with more than an "uh uh."

"Your husband is such a good man, so good-looking and so successful. You must try to work things out, you know. You are breaking God's commandments and will end up in hell. There's nothing worse than being a divorced woman and fallen from grace. Promise me you'll work it out. Will you?"

"I won't cry, I won't cry." I said to myself as my eyes flooded. Fortunately my lips were so numb they couldn't tremble. It didn't matter that the good little angel sitting on my right shoulder said, "It's O.K., Mary. You did the best you could." The dentist's words hurt, and I didn't like knowing that some people no longer thought of me as the good scout I thought myself. When I was growing up, my dad often said to me, "No matter what happens to you, Mary, no matter what people say to you, hold yourself gracefully, keep your chin up, your shoulders back and stand up straight." At least I could find a new dentist.

In spite of Henry VIII's making it legal in the Protestant

church to get divorced, trying to follow God's principles as they are described in the *Bible* is hard to do as a divorced Protestant woman. According to the person who wrote *Exodus*, God decreed, "Thou shalt not commit adultery." The priest of my church translated that to mean, "No sex with a married person who is not your spouse." Later, according to *Matthew*, Jesus added a gender-specific qualification, "Whosoever shall marry *her* that is divorced committeth adultery." There is no mention, however, of its being adultery when a divorced *man* marries a woman. And, what about that unfair bit that Abraham, Isaac and Jacob were allowed to have several wives, when women weren't allowed to have several husbands?

My grandmother, my mother and I were faced with the same choice. We could stay married and suffer the slow painful death of our personal dignity, or we could divorce our husbands and risk social ostracism. In spite of the fact that my *divorceé* grandmother was facing her future with a glass of Scotch in her hand, her parents were Christians in a broader sense of the word. "Our grandparents were really happy to have us," my Uncle Bobby told me. "Instead of putting us in the cottage, they gave us the main house and moved into the cottage themselves."

The Mediterranean-style home at 1230 North Arroyo Boulevard, on Pasadena's older west side, had three bedrooms and two baths. The guest cottage was at the end of a cobblestone walkway through grass which stayed green in the winter, unlike that in Chicago. I lived three blocks away from that house when my kids were teenagers. The house overlooks a wide, shallow canyon known as the Arroyo Seco, meaning *dry gully*, where the Rose Bowl football stadium is nestled.

Built in 1921, nine years before the Winters moved to California, the stadium seated 57,000 and was one of the first sports stadiums designed with parking facilities to accommodate a large quantity of automobiles. Eventually it was enlarged and now seats 100,000. Half a century later I would be a cheerleader, dressed in a short, red-and-white pleated skirt, kicking and screaming for the Pasadena High School football team in front of the bleachers there because the three high schools in Pasadena use the Rose Bowl for their home games.

Standing on the front lawn of the Winters' house looking over the Bowl, you can see the sweep of the San Gabriel foothills rising dramatically beyond the edge of the canyon. At night, the lights along the rim road across the canyon, about a quarter mile across, are a row of softly glowing orbs which my great grandfather likened to a string of pearls.

Dad and his brother Bobby adjusted quickly to the casual life of Southern California. They walked to their public school, hiked and explored the fissure canyons boring into the foothills farther up the arroyo and swam in the pool filled by a small waterfall at the end of the canyon, where you can still swim today.

What fascinated Dad most of all was the fluttering of Hollywood society in his grandmother's parlor. One evening, she was invited to the opening of a movie being shown at Grauman's Chinese Theater which has all the movie stars' handprints in front of it. Since she was unable to attend, she gave the tickets to her daughter and grandsons.

Dad told me about it. "Your Uncle Bobby and I were thrilled. In anticipation of seeing movie stars, we stashed small notepads and pencils in our pockets for autographs. But when we got out of the taxi Mom left us in the dust. Maybe she was embarrassed to be seen with two little kids. With those long legs of hers, she strode on up ahead of us. So we decided to play a trick on her. Looking around to make sure there were no real movie stars nearby, we ran up to our own mother with our notepads and pencils and asked her excitedly, 'Ma'am, ma'am, won't you give us your autograph?' Well, everyone around us thought our mother must be a movie star, so they gathered around her, too, asking for her autograph."

Dad's and Bobby's Aunt Rosemary had already started her career in Hollywood as the real thing. Her first part was in *Love on the Spot* in 1932. The year the boys moved to California she acted in *Mr. Quincey of Monte Carlo*, followed by three more movies in 1934. Then, in 1935 she landed her biggest role ever as the mother of Shirley Temple and wife of Joel McRae in the movie *Our Little Girl* but it wasn't much of a hit.

"It was about divorce," said Dad, "and divorce wasn't a very popular subject in the '30s. Rosemary was just one more woman who looked like Ginger Rogers and there was room for only one Ginger, and she could dance."

Nonetheless, having a beautiful movie star for an aunt in those days made Dad feel like royalty. When I was a little kid, he frequently dropped Hollywood names, most of which never meant anything to me. He kept track of their marriages and divorces as baseball fans keep track of home runs and box scores.

Eventually, Dad's mother found a cottage of her own on a little street called California Terrace. By this time Dad was in high school at Pasadena Junior College which then still included grades nine through twelve in addition to the first two years of college. Dad drove from the house on California Terrace straight down Colorado Boulevard to get there, following the same route the Rose Parade travels on New Year's Day today. Dad's memories of that part of his life were happy ones, though he said he was often reprimanded for being a troublemaker in school. My guess is that today he would be labeled ADD, which in my teaching days was called *hyperactive*.

He had lots of friends. One of them, Jerry, whose older sister hung out with my father and his friends in high school told me recently, "He was cheerful, outgoing, full of funny stories – and already eccentric."

As soon as he was sixteen, Dad bought himself a Model-T Ford and drove himself to school. He liked to sing when he drove. When I was little, he'd sing the first part of hit musical tunes, but he never seemed to finish one song before going on to another. I guess when his mood changed, the lyrics of whatever song he was singing changed, too. However, those musicals hadn't come out yet.

As he drove down Colorado, he didn't think anybody could hear him singing because the motor on his Model-T was so loud. But once at a Saturday night dance in a large ballroom over the Civic Center a girl came up to him and said, "I know who you are. I wait every morning at the bus stop on the corner of Fair Oaks and Colorado. I always know you are coming because I can hear you singing at the top of your voice in that old Model-T of yours."

It's been said there was smog in the San Gabriel Valley even when the Gabrielino Indians were the only residents there because the hills created a tight bowl that trapped the smoke from their fires. But my Aunt Kay, Uncle Bobby's wife, who grew up in the hills above the arroyo, told me, "In those days there was so little smog, we could often see Catalina Island more than twenty-six miles across the channel." I haven't seen that sight since I was sixteen, standing on my father's balcony in Santa Monica and that wasn't as far away.

To get away from the heat in the summers, residents of Pasadena went to the beach as often as possible. The Winters were among the first to build a tiny beach house in a private, now gated, community between Pasadena and San Diego called San Malo. The area has become one of those exclusive hideouts for old Pasadenans. All the cottages there were built in the style of San Malo in Normandy, where Grandfather Winter had attended university. I've often wondered if he influenced the building code. But the house he built was too small for his daughter Edith and her boys to stay in, so she rented a place up the coast in Laguna in Emerald Cove. Dad took my family to see it when I was young, telling us about his happy summers there and showing us the tidal pools among which he used to wander.

None of this made Edith any happier, however. "She still drank heavily when we first came to Pasadena," said Uncle Bobby. "Her speech would become slurry and she was often irritated. We thought it was our fault. Then one day she met this newspaperman from New York, your step-grandfather Paul McGinnis. He'd been a pilot during World War I and had just written a book about flying called *Lost Eden*. As you know, he told your grandmother to stop drinking. I know she didn't stop completely, but things got a lot better."

Paul bought his new family a house on Charlton Road in fashionable San Marino, Pasadena's southern neighbor, which enabled Bobby to attend the more prestigious South Pasadena High School the town fed. Since Dad was already at PJC, he stayed there.

"I liked Paul a lot," said my uncle, "but your dad wasn't so keen on him. He was very possessive of our mother and I think he viewed Paul as competition."

Soon after the move to San Marino, Dad's real father, Juny, pulled an uncharacteristic move, which Bud told me about later. Bud had just graduated from Shattuck Military Academy and bought a car, planning to drive out to California where he would be attending Stanford, but first he wanted to see his family.

"I'd written to the old man and told him what I was doing," Bud said. "When he got the letter, he wrote back saying he wanted to come along so he could see Tommy and Bobby. Then he sailed to New York and took a train to Minneapolis where I met up with him in my new car. We drove clear across the dessert with no air-conditioning and landed unexpectedly on the doorstep of my mother's and Paul's new house.

"Here we were having this unplanned reunion. I hadn't seen Mom in four years, and your dad and Bobby hadn't seen the old man for the same amount of time. Dad was horribly rude to Paul, whom I'd never met, and Mom wasn't all that civil to our old man. It was awkward all around."

Bobby, Nanna Adelaide, Bud and Dad

———◆———

CHAPTER NINETEEN

Shelter Island

While war devastated Europe during the summer of 1941, Dad and his brothers enjoyed an elegant life of leisure at their Nanna Adelaide's sprawling Shelter Island Victorian. The boys had taken the train there together from Pasadena. I suspect the insecurity of life overseas made Adelaide want to gather her family together in one place. Six months later Pearl Harbor was bombed.

All Adelaide's descendants attended the reunion: Juny with the boys, Aunt Rosemary with her daughter Julie, and Uncle John with his wife and three children. Recently I've come to know my Dad's cousin, Julie, who described that reunion. "Your father and I became good friends that summer. Something we had in common was that we hardly ever saw one of our parents. He was estranged from his father and I hardly knew my real mother, Rosemary. When she'd left my father and moved to Southern California to be an actress, I'd stayed in Chicago. My father remarried and I grew up calling my stepmother *Mother*. But Rosemary shipped me out for a visit for the opening of *Our Little Girl*. There was so much irony, sitting in that auditorium next to my real mother, watching her play mother to Shirley Temple in the movie, destined to divorce Shirley's father. I'm thinking, 'Why can't Rosemary be a real mother to me?'

"Since Bud was busy chasing this neighbor girl named Anita and Uncle John's kids were loads younger, I kicked around with your father and watched him and Bobby build a couple of surfboards. They got to be pretty good surfers, actually."

At the end of the summer the family dispersed, having no idea of how final the good-byes were to be. It was the last time the boys saw their grandmother, who would die in Chicago in 1948, and the last time Bud saw his father. Bobby and Dad would see him one more time. Everyone boarded the train for Grand Central where they would change directions for their particular destination. Julie returned to Chicago via the Twentieth Century Limited. She exchanged letters with Dad during the war but then they lost touch.

When the boys handed their luggage to the porter for the train back to California, he informed them that the surfboards were not allowed on board. Uncle Bobby told me, "Your father refused to leave them behind. He said he'd worked all summer on that thing, and it was going with him to California. He found the nearest newsstand and purchased a local paper in which he found a Model-A Ford Station wagon *Woody* listed for sale nearby. By the end of the day, he'd cashed in our train tickets and purchased the Woody. We strapped the two boards on top of the car and drove the 3,000-plus miles from New York to Pasadena. It was a miracle the Woody made it to the driveway of our home. Between the three of us boys, no one thought to check it for oil, and when I went to drive it to school the following day, it wouldn't start because the engine was completely melted."

Dad at a dance with a friend in the '40s

CHAPTER TWENTY

Manners and Movie Stars

My dad's move to Santa Monica after my parents' split gave him a chance to be closer to another passion besides the ocean. Next to the public beach in front of his building were the privately owned sands of the exclusive clubs and homes of the movie stars. In a sense, his new mansion was right there in line with the rest. He'd arrived. Now he could continue preparing his children for our part in his play.

About a year after the move, he announced to the three of us that he wanted to take us to Perino's in Beverly Hills for lunch. There were several reasons for his wanting to do this. None of them were to sample the world-famous food or appreciate their collection of fine wines. That would have cost real money.

He wanted a chance to star-gaze. But the real reason we were going to one of the Sunset Strip's most celebrated restaurants in our Sunday-best clothes on a day when our friends in Pasadena were attending Little League games was to practice eating soup correctly and learn how to use a finger bowl.

Back during the days when our family was together, Dad's Grandmother Alice's old finger bowls hid in the dark depths of the highest dish cabinet, which I could reach only by standing on a kitchen chair. They were of crystal glass, with small violets etched around the sides, used regularly by Alice perhaps, but since then only collecting dust.

We'd seen them used, when I was around eleven, Tom ten and Charlie seven. Mom ceremoniously brought five of them to the table on a silver tray one evening after a meal of baby-back ribs. A sliver of lemon floated on the water in each one.

"What kind of soup is that?" Charlie had said, bending his head down until his nose almost got wet. "It looks like water."

"It is water," said Dad. "These are finger bowls, so you can wash your hands without getting up from the table." He acted as if it were as usual as passing the salt.

Both of Charlie's hands were in the bowl, and water was being flung across his placemat before my parents realized his intentions. Their chairs screeched as they both jumped up and simultaneously dove for Charlie yelling, "Noooo."

"Put your hands back in your lap right this minute, young man," said Dad.

With Charlie's shoulders back in line, a five-minute lesson began on how to hold our fingers together tightly, as if they were in the face of a puppet, dip them into the water without touching the sides of the bowl, rub the fingers tenderly together as if we were dusting sand off our finger tips, and dry them daintily with our napkins.

I thought that was the end of finger bowls and that we wouldn't have to deal with them again until we ate with the Queen, but Dad didn't think the impression he'd made on us was deep enough.

Perino's Restaurant was across from a huge hotel with the

same name as the hotel by the apartment in Chicago where Dad grew up: the Ambassador. It was set off the boulevard with a long curved driveway lined with palm trees. Dad pointed to it as we drove into the parking lot. "They used to have a big night-club there called the Coconut Grove," he said, with a dreamy look on his face, as if he wished he were back in the dancing days of his youth. The pink and black of Perino's walls and leather booths made me think we still were.

"Don't order a main dish," said Dad as soon as we'd handed our jackets to the *maître d'*, settled into our booth, and he'd scanned the room looking for Steve McQueen and Fay Dunaway. We'd been given huge menus, big enough to be room screens. I might as well have been back in Italy because none of the items on the list were in English.

"Then, what's the point of coming here?" said Tommy.

"Don't argue with me, Tommy. Charlie, get your elbows off the table! We're going to have soup and dessert and I'm going to have a plate of Dungeness crab."

I would have preferred a toasted peanut-butter sandwich with potato chips. The word *soup* wasn't on the menu. Neither were prices. When I asked why there weren't any prices on the menu, Dad proudly explained, "Because in fine restaurants they only give the menus with prices to the host of the party or to the men, so the women don't have to worry about the cost of things." I could see he was happy he'd had a chance to tell me that important fact before The Prince took me out for the Big Date.

The minestrone soup was presented in low flat bowls, like those we'd used in Europe, but which weren't commonly seen in the U.S. yet. When the waiter placed it in front of me, I noticed he turned the dish carefully to make sure the Perino's logo was facing me. Dad always made me do that at home with the fleur-de-lis on his grandmother's china.

"Now remember," said Dad, so loudly that I glanced at the people next to us to see if they heard it too, "Drink out of the side of the spoon, not the front of it. And don't slurp, Charlie! No noise.

"Good. Now when you get to the bottom of the bowl, remember to tip it away from you and scoop out of the back of the bowl. Don't tip it towards you. A gentleman wouldn't want the soup to spill down the front of his jacket." Dad was wearing his black wedding suit with a red tie. His white shirt was pressed and he looked quite handsome. I tried to picture him in a tuxedo.

As my brothers and I ate wedges of chocolate cake and Dad enjoyed his crab, the peaceful calm was only punctured now and then with his demonstrations on how to break the crab meat out of its shell. However, when he finished and the waiter brought him his finger bowl, he wanted to make sure we were fully alert.

"See, kids, this is what they do at the best restaurants. Now, watch." This time I didn't need to look to see heads turning at the next table.

That was probably the last elegant meal my father ever had, and it wasn't even a full one. He wasn't there a few months later when I went on a date with a real *prince charming* to see his etiquette lessons weren't wasted.

Summer of 1972

CHAPTER TWENTY-ONE

The Castle Starts to Crumble

Rent from twenty-eight apartments on the Pacific Ocean should have given Dad a steady income, but the building was never full. He wasn't able to maintain a good relationship with his tenants and they often moved as soon as their lease was up. Even though he thought he was being friendly and hospitable, that wasn't the case.

One weekend when I was visiting, he came to greet me at the parking lot when a new tenant, George Penderhost, walked by carrying laundry to his car. My dad stopped him and said, "I saw the moving vans yesterday. Did everything fit all right in your apartment?"

"Sure, it all fits fine," George said, "but, I'll need to buy a clothes bureau to store all my shirts and stuff. They're spread all over the floor. I've kind of run out of cash for the moment, but I'll get to it soon."

The next day we were out back again. I was reading a maga-zine in a porch chair while Dad swept the area around the trash bins. Another tenant, Alice Shift, came out of the back door of the building dragging a four-drawer bureau she'd painted pink with green trim, parking it by the bins before Dad could drop his broom and help her. On top of the bureau was a large note which read, "GOODWILL."

"Don't you want that bureau?" asked Dad.

"No," said Alice. "My aunt gave me a nicer one and I don't need this one any more. Besides, I'm tired of pink and green."

"You could strip the paint off and it would be a handsome piece," said Dad.

"I suppose so, but that sounds like a lot of work. Besides, there isn't any more room in my place for it, anyway."

When Alice went inside, Dad looked the bureau over, pulling out the drawers to see if they slid smoothly on their tracks and tapping the wood to see what kind it was. He left the drawers in a stack on the pavement, lessening the weight of the bureau, and hefted the mainframe into his arms. Then he nudged open the door with his knee, and disappeared in the direction Alice had come. Several minutes later he reappeared empty-handed, lifted the stack of drawers and went back inside again. In a few minutes he came out with a satisfied look and returned to his sweeping.

The following morning I found a note at the foot of the door of the Mezzanine, which must have been slipped under the previous evening. It read. "Dear Tom, I assume you left the pink bureau in my apartment. I appreciate the gesture, but I'm not too fond of pink and green. I've left the bureau for the Salvation Army out by the trash. If there is anyone else who wants it, you can give it away. Sincerely, George #205."

I handed the note to my father. As he read it, his face began to redden and puff up and when he finished, he angrily threw it into the trash. Then he stormed out of the loft. Later, on my way to my car, I could see the bureau where George had left it. Only Dad had scribbled over the words Salvation Army, "Unwanted gift by thankless tenant. Remove immediately or it will be thrown into the trash."

From then on, whenever I was with Dad and we saw George, Dad's face turned into an ugly scowl. If George said, "Hi, Tom," he wouldn't answer but would turn his face and walk the other direction. George was gone by the next summer.

Since his days as a nurseryman, Dad had collected potted palms. When he and my mother sold the greenery in Pasadena, he moved them to an area on his parking lot, creating a miniature tropical forest. Dad spent most hot summer afternoons watering the pots. The only evidence he was in the middle of his mini-jungle was the tail made by the green hose leading out of the palms to the waterspout. Most of Dad's tenants returned home from work at the end of a long commute anxious to get from their cars to the peace and quiet of their apartments. However, the path from one to the other went directly past the jungle.

Dad, who had been home alone all day, looked forward to the return of his tenants. Often at the end of hot summer days, he sat in his patio chair in the shade of his palm trees, sometimes wearing no shirt and perspiring heavily from working in the sun. Since he'd finished with his hose, it no longer indicated his presence. When a tenant strolled by, Dad was like the troll under the bridge in *Billy Goats Gruff*, jumping out to greet them.

"Hey there, Susan, did you see they were filming a movie on PCH today?"

"No, I was …"

"There were three changing-room trucks, one of them parked right in front of our building. The cameras were set up on the beach and I talked to the crew for a while. They said …"

Susan tried to participate in the conversation, perhaps to say she was late for her date with her boyfriend and needed to dash, but Dad's booming voice bulldozed her attempts.

In another instance, after Dad mentioned to me that his tenant Ted Sotherby had missed two rent payments in a row, I saw Dad taping a note to Mr. Sotherby's door. It was already covered with torn notebook paper scraps and bits of newspaper with writing down the narrow blank edges in Dad's handwriting. One said, "Dear Sotherby, In case you can't read, sign on front door reads Apartments, not Bank. Request you take care of responsibility and remove yourself immediately. Management." Another said, "Dear Mr. Good-for-Nothing. Herewith request payment in full and your immediate departure from premises. This is not a charity. Management."

In one instance, which my Uncle Bobby related to me recently, Dad's appeals for justice backfired. "Your father was increasingly annoyed by the trash which collected in front of his building on Pacific Coast Highway." Bobby said. "Chautauqua Boulevard, as it runs into the highway there, creates the county line and Pacific Coast Highway is the responsibility of the state. The city's street sweepers ignored your father's place completely, so he appealed to the county sanitation department. When the county wouldn't do anything about it, your father scooped up a shoebox full of gum wrappers, dry leaves and other dry debris and sent it by post to then Governor of California, Ronald Reagan. A week later, a state trooper came to his door. 'Mr. Ames, your package was not appreciated,' the trooper said. 'We aren't going to do this again now are we?' Your father finished this story to me by saying that if Nancy Reagan sent the package back to him C.O.D., he'd have been sure not to accept it."

Dad and me behind his apartment house — 1972

CHAPTER TWENTY-TWO

Wheaton

I left California and my regular visits with Dad to attend Wheaton, an all-women's liberal arts college in Massachusetts. Dad wrote me every month or so. The letters were much longer than those from my mother, and he kept himself informed of what classes I was taking and whether I dated anyone, which Mom didn't. The only vacation I went home for was Christmas.

Every spring Wheaton held a father-daughter weekend, which I dreaded. Fathers in fashionable sport coats and ties showed up for cocktails in the president's garden on Friday evening, followed by a candlelight dinner. On Saturdays, father-and-daughter tennis matches were held. Girls affectionately linked arms with their doting fathers and walked here and there around the campus grounds and pond, having a wonderful time. They visited the gallery to see the art we'd produced and on Saturday nights everyone got dressed up and went in large groups to the fancier restaurants, either in Boston or Providence. On Sundays, the fathers attended church where the student chorus sang their best. I would have preferred missing a dead father to the feelings I had.

Every year I would send Dad the invitation, hoping he wouldn't accept. I couldn't hurt his feelings by excluding him. Yet, if he had come, I would have felt ashamed of the way he dressed. He had not bought a new suit in decades, and his boisterous and gruff manner tended to put people off. So if he'd come, I would have spent the three days worrying he was going to do something unexpected that would embarrass me. Fortunately, he couldn't afford the trip; if he could have, he would have been there. The situation was probably painful for him, too. If I hadn't been part of some of the performances being held on campus, I would have left on those weekends and maybe visited a relative nearby. Instead, I spent the days in my dorm room feeling sorry for myself and attended the dinners my friends and their fathers organized.

━━━◆━━━

When I returned home for the summer between my sophomore and junior year, I noticed there were no tenents residing in Dad's building. He never discussed his finances with me; however, it was easy to deduce he was running out of money. A large painting he'd inherited from his grandmother, and some smaller artwork he'd been proud of, were missing. I also suspected he was selling the family silver, but when I asked him if he needed help, his answer was, "Of course not. We Puritans can always make do." I could see by the look on his face I'd offended him.

Charlie, the only one of us children who hadn't left for college, finally explained what had been going on while I was away. "The fire department slapped Dad with a heavy fine for not complying with the fire code," he said. "When he didn't pay the fine, the fire department notified the remaining tenants they had to leave, which they did. Dad retaliated by changing all the locks on the building so no one would let the fire inspectors in. Trouble was, when the meter reader came from the Department of Water and Power, he couldn't get in either. So they billed Dad for more than he was used to.

"When I visited him that weekend, I found him in a huffy mood. He was pacing in circles and mumbling about something. I couldn't understand a word he was saying. When he saw me come through the door of the Mezzanine he pounced on me, 'I want you to come with me to the DWP,' he said.

"'Whatever for?' I said.

"'I need a witness,' he said.

"I knew the conversation would be a lot shorter if I didn't try to reason with him.

"I returned to Chautauqua Monday morning and drove Dad to the DWP building in downtown Los Angeles. A young gentleman was working the customer service window. When Dad thrust his bill under the gentleman's nose and shook it violently, the man shrank back.

"'What's this?' Dad said loudly. 'What's this bill for?'

"'Let me take a look at it, sir,' said the agent, regaining his composure. 'Let's see what the matter is. It says here access to the meter was denied. Did you ...'

"'Excuse me, excuse me,' Dad yelled. 'That is my private property. No one goes on my property without my permission.' He grabbed the bill out of the agent's hands and shook it in his face again.

"'Sir, we must have access,' the agent tried to say.

"'Excuse me, excuse me,' Dad said again. His voice was shaking and his face darkening from red to plum purple. 'What's this charge for? What's this bill all about?'

"Every time the agent tried to talk, Dad interrupted him,

saying, 'Excuse me. Excuse me.' But then he started saying things like, "I know you were there. You were all there. You were all there when they came.'

"I tugged at Dad's arm and said, 'Dad, let's go. They couldn't read your meter because the door was locked.'

"He threw off my hand. 'You were all there. You were watching me,' he said.

That's when we knew Dad was *losing it*.

He began to inhabit the whole building himself, reasoning that if it were a single-family residence, he wouldn't have to follow the decrees of the big, bad fire department. Piece by piece, the family hand-me-down furniture left the Mezzanine and settled into the empty apartments. One of the single-bedroom units became his dining room. He placed a heavy, ornately carved mahogany library table that he'd bought with the Big House in the center of the former living room. Then he surrounded it with a hodgepodge of his mother's dining room chairs and two high-backed wooden benches he'd scavenged. The effect was strangely medieval and I imagined he was becoming the lord of a dilapidated castle, like Beauty's Beast.

When he proudly showed the room to me, I asked him if he was going to block off the adjoining kitchenette and bathroom. His answer was a simple shrug of the shoulders which I understood to mean, "What do you mean kitchenette and bathroom? Just look the other way and pretend they aren't there."

———◆———

Wheaton was a very *preppy* school at the time. It seemed to me that over seventy-five percent of the students had attended private high schools, which I had not, and the wealthier girls who'd been to the same schools or been debutantes in the same town stuck together in tightly knit groups. One clique from Ohio tended to gather in a room down the hall from me and spent more time playing bridge, drinking and smoking than studying, which seemed a lot more fun than my life. Often their laughing voices wafted into my room in the wee hours of the morning.

One evening I overheard them talking about their spring vacations. What particularly caught my ear were the words, "Harbour Island" and "Bahamas." I listened more intently and discovered that one girl named Bessie had a vacation home on the island where my grandfather had lived. The next day as we were walking to our classes I hurried to catch up with her.

"Excuse, me, Bessie," I called.

She turned around at her name, but didn't seem pleased it was I using it. "Yes?"

"I'm Mary, I live right down the hall from you. I heard you have a place on Harbour Island."

"Yeah?"

"Well, I know this is a strange question, but my grandfather lived there, and I never met him and I was just wondering if you might have run across him."

She gave me a look which I interpreted as meaning, "And who do you think you are that you might possibly know anyone I know?"

"What's his name?" she said.

"Knowlton Lyman Ames."

"No. Sorry."

"Well, he may have been known as Snake." I ventured.

"Snake? Snake?" she said excitedly. "Your grandfather was Snake? He practically lived at our house. I loved that guy. He used to own a chicken ranch and he would come in, leaving feathers and seeds in a trail behind him all over the carpet. I used to sit on his knee. He was this really fun old man who would tell me all these stories. He and my dad went fishing together and were always telling fish stories and talking about the old days in Chicago. I can't believe it. He's your grandfather?"

"Yeah," I said, feeling as if now I was invited to finish the conversation.

"What did you mean you never met him?"

"He and my father didn't talk to each other. My father just called him the Mystery Man, but he wrote me a few times at the end of his life."

"I have to tell my mother," Bessie said. "She'll die."

By that time we'd reached our classroom building.

The next week was Easter Break. On the Monday morning after everyone returned and I was walking to my first class, it was Bessie who tried to catch up with me. "Mary, I told my mother about you. She's dying to meet you. Where do you live?"

Since I drove my car across country every summer, to and from school, we arranged for a stopover in Ohio the following June.

Bessie lived in Shaker Heights, a day's trip from Massachusetts. I had never visited horse country before. Their driveway was longer than most of the entrances to the chateaux I'd seen in France. The electric gate was already open. When the uniformed maid let me in, she explained that Bessie and her parents were out riding. "You can wait here in the library, if you want. They'll be returning shortly. Can I get you anything to drink?"

I sat down in the depths of a dark leather chair surrounded by paintings and photos of horses. Outside the windows, lush woods without any other buildings extended as far as I could see. Bessie and her mother finally came in and greeted me. "This is Mary, Mother."

"We are so excited to meet Snake's granddaughter, Mary.

What a wonderful surprise."

We gathered at a dining table, big enough to seat twelve, for a formal lunch. I picked up a silver fork that weighed three times as much as my mother's silver forks and it seemed to be twice as large. Once the servants had cleared the dessert plates, Bessie's mother fetched a huge scrapbook with clippings about my grandfather and placed it on the table.

Everything looked similar to what I'd seen before in photos of my father when he was little on the island: people dressed in khakis by palm trees. There were lots of newspaper articles featuring Bessie's family written by my grandfather in *Harbour Island Nowadays*. As I read them, I wondered how my life might have been different if my dad and his father had remained friendly towards each other. Would I have been as fond of my grandfather as Bessie was? Had it been his relationship with Bessie that prompted him to write to me?

I reached home that summer a few days earlier than I expected. When my brothers and I went to see Dad the next day, we didn't call ahead as we usually did, assuming he wouldn't mind and would be happy to see us. After leaving my car in his parking lot, we walked through the palm jungle and knocked on the back door. Even after several loud pounds with my brother Tom's fist, and calling out Dad's name, there was no answer.

"Maybe he went down the street to the liquor store," suggested Charlie. We walked to the small shop on Pacific Coast Highway where Dad occasionally bought beer and simple groceries, but we could easily see Dad wasn't there when we arrived. At the counter the clerk was giving change to a teenage boy.

"Do you know who Tom Ames is?" my brother asked when the

man looked up at us.

"Sure," he said, curtly.

"Has he been in today?" I asked.

"I haven't seem Tom in several months."

As he was talking, I could see Charlie's point to a cork board on the wall behind him. It was papered with layers of bad bank checks, speared together by multi-colored push-pins like shishka-bobs. Charlie said, "Look at that yellow one."

On close inspection I realized it was a familiar Security Pacific Bank check with our father's bold signature on it and there were several more just like it.

The man smiled when he saw the realization appear on my face. "Well, thanks anyway," I said.

"Yeah. See ya," said Charlie as we left the store.

We finally found Dad, walking along the beach. He was happy to see us, but we didn't mention our visit to the liquor store.

———— ◆ ————

Dad told me he wouldn't be attending my graduation from Wheaton because it would be too awkward for him with my mother there. I knew, of course, he couldn't buy a plane ticket. However, I found a small parcel from him waiting in my post office box on the big day.

As I tore off the brown paper, I fully expected a hand-me-down gift such as the gold bracelet that had been his mother's which he'd given me the previous Christmas or the opal brooch I'd received for my birthday which had belonged to my Grandmother Alice. I hadn't received anything newly purchased in years. Apparently his pockets weren't completely empty, however, because inside a new jewelry box was a glittering set of one-carat-diamond earring posts. My dad was still full of surprises.

My wedding day, September 7, 1974

CHAPTER TWENTY-THREE

Celebrations

Returning to Pasadena after Wheaton, I enrolled in the graduate program at the University of Southern California to obtain my teaching credential, taking classes at night and working as a student teacher during the daytime. My mother set me up in my own apartment on the west side of Pasadena near the Huntington Hotel. I shared this with a woman named Gail who was attending the same program at USC. We'd been friends since high school. Dad liked her instantly. Her father and my father had known each other in high school, also.

I tried to see Dad at least once a month, driving out for the day, or simply going out to dinner with him, but there were no more overnight stays.

We had a better time together when he came to visit me. He enjoyed helping Gail and me set up our new apartment and always arrived with his Falcon station wagon loaded with plants. Soon we had our own mini jungle of raphis and chameadora palms on our patio. Dad showed us how to make cuttings from the creeping

Charlie plants and brought us pots of wandering-jew and a shade plant with very tall leaves called aspidistra. "Those are cast iron plants," he said, "You can't kill them."

Finding furnitue other people undervalued became a game for us. For $25 at the Salvation Army he purchased a Victorian oak chest to hold our dishes. At a yard sale he pointed out an oak bureau hiding under years of chipped paint and showed me how to strip it and restore the wood with oil.

———

My connection to my father was like a fraying electric wire. One moment it worked and the next moment I was surprised by a short. No sooner was I finding something we liked to do together and hoping Dad was back on the road to normality than a new event reminded me we weren't.

As Christmas rolled around and Gail made plans to go home with her family, I realized it was my first chance as an independent adult to entertain my own family at my own place. I was under the illusion that if I were in charge of the celebration, I could make it a cheerful holiday again. My brothers and father agreed to come to my apartment for Christmas Eve.

I was harried, because I had just finished a set of exams for graduate school, but I figured out how to roast a turkey, mash potatoes and steam string beans. I set the table with the inherited plates and damask napkins Dad had given me and lit candles everywhere. I bought Coke for my brother Charlie, a six-pack of beer for Dad and Tommy, and a bottle of champagne for all of us to drink with dessert.

Dad showed up smelling very good and wearing clean clothes, though they were wrinkled. I gave him a beer and he went around looking my place over and pulling dead leaves off my plants on the patio. So far so good. When my brothers showed up, having driven from my mother's where they were staying for the holidays, I gave Charlie his Coke, Tommy his beer and then we sat down for dinner. We were never a family of small talkers.

As the beers disappeared, so did the turkey, pretty much in silence. While I served the pumpkin pie, someone made the mistake of asking Dad how things were going at the apartment house. That tiny spark blazed into a big fire. When my brothers tried to calm Dad down, he got up and went home. Shrugging their shoulders, Tommy and Charlie put on their jackets and went back to Mom's. I sat back down at my little dining table decorated with the hopes of a successful evening, opened the bottle of champagne, and drank the whole thing. For the first time in my twenty-two years, I went to bed drunk.

Then in January Dad did a nice thing. I was offered a full-time teaching position in the school where I'd been a student-teacher. It was part of the Pasadena Unified School district in which I'd grown up and the secretary happened to be the mother of a friend I'd had in elementary school. So she knew all about my dad and the Purple Cow House. Entering the school office on the first day of my new job, she handed me a huge bouquet of flowers, "These came for you early this morning," she said with a smile. The gift card said, "Go, tiger. You'll be a great teacher. Love, Dad"

That summer I planned my wedding to a fellow I'd dated in high school after Rick. This man only tolerated Dad, calling him the Black Sheep, and Dad didn't like him much either. My Uncle Bud told me years later that Dad had said, "It will never work. He is too much like me."

The wedding was to be in September. It was 1974 and the hippie era when weddings were still do-it-yourself affairs was mostly behind us. Ceremonies had moved back inside the churches from the meadows, and brides wore shoes again. I still planned to wear wreaths of flowers on my hair instead of a veil and I sewed my own wedding dress, as did my bridesmaids. But I dreaded the day, wondering if Dad would make a scene.

He didn't. He told me ahead of time he'd take me down the aisle but not attend the reception which was to be at my mother's house. There would be no father-daughter dance. He let my mother pay the bills without a fuss, but when he arrived at the church on the big day wearing his black wedding suit, he lugged a four-foot-wide wine-barrel planter filled with a gorgeous clump of raphis palms as a present for the minister. And when he looked into my eyes with his big smile and extended his arm to lead me to my new life, I was very happy he was there.

Chautauqua apartment building from Pacific Coast Highway

CHAPTER TWENTY-FOUR

The Lawyers and the Bank

With time, my visits with my father became shorter and less frequent. Conversations had become completely one-sided and were simply too difficult to enjoy. He asked plenty of questions, but his attention didn't stick around for the answer. My brothers, husband and I were weary of hearing him vent about the unresponsive city and how "Public Enemy Number One," our mother, was turning us children against him.

When we did see him, it was usually just for dinner. His driver's license had been taken away for a reason he wouldn't tell us, so one of us had to pick him up at Chautauqua. His favorite restaurant was called the Belle Vue where he liked the pork chops with applesauce. Less elegant than Perino's, it was also a great place for spotting movie stars.

Seldom could we sustain a happy note in our conversations. With each beer he ordered, his voice level went up, the red flush darkened in his face, the shake in his hands increased, and the thread of his thoughts became harder and harder to follow. I was always relieved when the evening was over and we could take him home.

Nonetheless, I still believed things would turn around and get better one day and bought into his promises that when his enemies stopped bothering him he would be happy again.

I was having a hard time financially myself. I could hardly make ends meet with my teaching salary and my husband's business venture never became profitable. He and I argued repeatedly about money, trying to stretch what we had to fit our needs. I was afraid if my father couldn't straighten his life out, he would come to me for help and I didn't know what I would do. I should have known better. No matter how hard things became for Dad, he would never lean on me.

In 1976, my husband folded his enterprise and enrolled in the business school at Stanford. I found a new teaching job and we moved north to Palo Alto. A part of me was relieved to be an eight-hour drive away from my father, though I realized I was just hiding. Since Dad was no longer driving and couldn't afford transportation to visit me, I saw him only at Christmas and maybe once during the summer, but it made me sad that he didn't see the way I redesigned the small garden in the new house, or the additions I'd made to my collection of oak furniture.

After my husband's two-year course ended, we returned to Pasadena and purchased a family-sized house on beautiful, tree-lined Madison Avenue. I expected to see Dad more often, but I didn't. He called me only every other month or so and – I'm ashamed to admit now – that was fine with me. When I became pregnant, I hoped that having Dad's first grandchild would be something he and I could enjoy together. I remembered how he relished being a father when I was little and thought he might feel the same about being a grandfather. As soon as I found out I was pregnant, I called him and announced the news. He seemed pleased and we talked again about a month later. Then we didn't communicate for a while.

At the end of my eighth month, I received a phone call from an attorney in Beverly Hills. "Are you related to Thomas W. Ames?" the attorney asked. He'd introduced himself as Mr. Vinnie Rathberg.

I hadn't spoken to Dad in six months. A wrench of shame mixed with anxiety tightened around my stretched stomach and the use of Dad's formal name made me suspect a nuisance, such as a sales call.

"He's my father."

"Are you aware of the fact that he hasn't been paying his mortgage payments, and that the bank foreclosed on the apartment building he owned on Chautauqua Boulevard in Santa Monica?"

The wrench on my stomach cranked up another notch.

"I have no knowledge of my father's business affairs," I said. "What can I do for you, sir?"

"Do you know how we can reach your father?" he asked.

"No," I said, realizing that Dad wasn't sitting in front of his television in his Mezzanine where he should have been. "Does he know he's been foreclosed upon?"

"Yes, he certainly does," Mr. Rathberg said. 'Look, I can't really discuss the details with you. He just disappeared a couple of months ago. He left all his personal belongings in the apartment building and we don't know what to do with them."

I was thinking to myself that I'd turned into a real jerk. Here I was learning that my dad had lost his home and I'd been completely unaware of it. I was ashamed I'd been enjoying my emotional vacation from him and hadn't done anything about returning from it. I was also worried. It wasn't like Dad to abandon his possessions.

The family antiques were more important to him than I was.

"I'm sorry," I said. "The last I knew, Dad was living in his apartment building. He has not told me about this and I have no idea where he might have gone. I haven't seen him in several months. What do you have to do with this?"

"Well, I represent the development firm which bought your father's building from the bank. You need to understand we are being extremely generous here. We are under no obligation to return anything left in that apartment house. We could just throw it all away, but there are a lot of personal items and antique pieces of furniture we thought would be of importance to Mr. Ames."

I was young and inexperienced, but I knew what my dad would have said about Mr. Rathberg. "That ... is full of baloney." I pictured the furniture in all those apartments and the piles of junk Dad salvaged when tenants moved out and left things behind. I wondered who was taking care of the palm jungle. Where could Dad be?

"How did you find me?" I asked.

"A letter from you was found in a box of things Mr. Ames left behind. Your name and address in Pasadena were on the return address of an envelope containing a letter addressed to 'Dad.' We called information for Pasadena and here you are."

As I pictured this stranger rummaging through my father's personal belongings, I was having a hard time thinking straight. It was ninety-five degrees and smoggy, a typical day for Pasadena in late May. I could feel the heat under the twenty pounds of baby on my front side, and my house had no central air conditioning.

"I don't know what to do," I told Mr. Rathberg, truthfully. "What did Dad leave behind?"

"I can't tell you precisely. Some nice furniture and file cabinets containing personal records."

There were several pieces of furniture I knew my father wouldn't sell. All the antiques had family stories behind them. My dad slept in the Chippendale bed that used to be the baron's and the Jacobean chest came to America on one of the ships during the first Great Migration. Dad designed the living room around his grandmother's mahogany highboy as if it had been an altar. My brothers and I were told repeatedly that the heavy, ornately carved, claw-footed Federal desk had been shipped around Cape Horn over a century ago by an ocean steamer.

But the piece Dad prized most was an old, stained and pitted, gate-leg table. Pasted in the bottom of its single drawer was a sheet of yellowed parchment paper on which was written an appraisal of the table in a beautiful calligraphic hand which must have been written a century earlier when my great-grandparents commissioned the appraisal. It stated that the table was made before the Revolution out of cherry wood. The day he showed me the inside of the drawer, Dad was so excited you'd have thought he'd found a diamond ring hiding in a crevice. It was as if the age and history of the table validated the social standing he'd lost years earlier.

"We really don't have to give these things to anyone," Mr. Rathberg was repeating, "but seeing as they belonged to your family, my client is offering to give them back to you."

I didn't hear any sincerity or charity in his voice. I wondered what the catch was. "Well, how about if my husband and I go down there and take a look?" I said.

"I'm afraid you can't do that. You see, your father owes my client some money."

The wrench cranked even tighter as Mr. Rathberg continued, "My client is willing to give back the furniture, but he needs some assurance you will take responsibility for your father."

"I think I'd better talk to my husband and call you back." I was having a hard time breathing.

"We'll only hold on to these things for a few more days. My client is trying to clean out the building. If we can't agree, he'll haul everything away and sell it to pay off part of the debt." He sounded like a used-car salesman.

"You mean, we have to pay back the money my father owes?" Fear was turning into panic.

"No, but we'd like a deposit to show you aren't taking the furniture and running away with it. We need to know your actions are in the interest of your father."

"What do you want?" I asked. I felt like a robot doomed to follow orders it wasn't allowed to understand.

"The furniture has been collected in an area of the large room on the bottom floor of the building. We'd like you to take everything. It may take a couple of moving vans just to fit the plants. There are quite a few of them, you know. You will also be required to clean up any mess left behind. That was to be your father's responsibility. I would like to draft an agreement which states you have taken possession of the furniture and belongings so when your father returns we will have proof we tried to dispose of these belongings in a responsible manner."

After writing down the rest of the details, I hung up the phone and remained sitting in my chair gazing at the note. I'd been coping with a loopy dad all my life. Normally I had been able to rise to the occasion and take care of things, but not that day. "Would it be asking too much, God, for you to make my interactions with my father more timely and less confusing?" I prayed. Then to the open air, where I pictured my vanished father, I yelled, "Where are you? And what in heaven's name do you want me to do with this damn lawyer?"

I considered calling my mother who lived three miles away at the other end of Pasadena. Then I remembered that for the past fifteen years she'd been trying to stuff Dad into the deepest hole of her past, no matter how expensive her weekly therapy was. The mere mention of his name turned her as cold and stiff as a statue.

Abandoning that idea, I thought about talking to my husband. Since I was not looking forward to telling him that his sense of family obligation was about to be tested, I decided to wait until he came home from work. I weighed the idea of discussing the problem with my two brothers who lived on the opposite coast, one in Buffalo, and the other in Vermont, but they seemed pretty remote from the problem at hand. Finally, sick of holding my head up and being brave for the moment, I did what I really wanted to do. I sat on the couch in my living room with my arms around my great big stomach and burst into tears.

In the end, my mother and my husband helped me organize a rescue of Dad's possessions from the building. Mom lent me the money Mr. Rathberg had requested and my husband accompanied me to his offices in Beverly Hills. I signed the release papers and handed over the cashier's check. When I got home, I gave Bekins Moving Company a call, requesting they send two vans and a clean-up crew to the Chautauqua building several days later. My husband and I then cleared out space in our garage in Pasadena to store the furniture. For the plants, we erected a hundred-foot-long wooden platform over our driveway covered by green plastic material to shade them from the summer sun. Actually, my husband did most of the work. I was now in my ninth month and could barely move.

We still knew nothing of Dad's whereabouts. When we went to his building we found, as reported, his stuff gathered in the center of the retail space on the first floor. The prized antiques were there, along with several legal file cabinets overflowing with folders and boxes of papers I wouldn't bother to sort until years later. There were also several rooms worth of miscellaneous junk furniture tenants had left behind that I had never seen before.

It took most of a blistering hot Saturday to load the moving vans. The jungle filled one and a third of the second. As the trucks drove away, the cleaning crew began sweeping up the rubbish and dust from the retail space. I went down to the retail unit, at the opposite end of the building from the parking lot, to do a final checkup, like a good Brownie, making sure we were leaving things better than we found them, when my husband walked into the room looking spooked. He'd just been overseeing the cleanup of the parking lot. Crossing over the freshly swept concrete floor to me he whispered, "Your dad is here."

"Where?"

"He's up on the parking lot. He looks awful."

"Where's he been?"

"I don't know. You'd better go talk to him."

I waddled up the short hill to the parking lot level. Rounding the corner of the building I could see him by the back door where his jungle had been, sweeping its remains with a long-handled push broom. I'd never seen him thinner. Two knobby knees jutted through frayed holes in his baggy pants. His black wing-tips were molded to the odd shapes of his size twelve-and-a-half feet and beyond hope of being polished back to health. His hair stood out in ornery, uneven tufts, like the steel wool he used to refinish salvaged furniture. The thick lenses of his glasses were cracked and covered with yellowing cellophane tape. One bow was held to the frame with a safety pin. He didn't even look up as I called to him. It was as if he were just part of the cleaning crew doing his job. He had a look of servitude where I expected anger or a mischievous smile.

"Dad! Hi! How are you? Where have you been?" I asked as I approached.

He still didn't look up. He didn't say, "Hi, honey. Good to see you," or "Where's my stuff?" or "What are you doing?" He just seemed to know all about it as if he'd been a fly on the wall watching the whole thing during the last week. "I was in the hospital," he said sullenly.

"We didn't know where you were. I didn't know what to do with all your stuff!" It was hard for me to hold back the desperation and frustration from my voice.

"Where is it going?" he asked.

"To our garage. I had no place else to put it. What did you want me to do with it?"

"That's okay for now. I'll check it out later." He continued to watch his broom move the dirt along the pavement.

I left him there and finished directing and paying off the cleaning crew. It was dusk when the truck left the driveway and the cooling air coming from the ocean was extremely welcome. The only place left to sit down was the retaining wall of the parking lot along Chautauqua Boulevard. My stomach stuck out between my aching legs. I felt sticky and dusty and wished I had something cold to drink. My husband and my father walked over and sat next to me.

"When will the things get delivered to your house?" Dad finally asked.

My husband answered, "Not until tomorrow morning." Both of us were dreading the unloading process. "Do you want to come up to Pasadena with us?"

"No," Dad said. You'd have thought aliens would destroy him if he entered Pasadena again. He hadn't seen our new house.

"Where are you living?" I asked.

"I'm staying in this place across town. I was having coffee at Norm's and this guy and his wife, who often come by for breakfast when I'm there, heard me say I was getting kicked out of my building. They own a warehouse where they store something or other and there's a small caretaker's unit on the property. They said if I were willing to keep an eye on the property, I could stay in the unit. So that's where I've been when I wasn't in the hospital."

"Shall we go get some dinner?" I said. "We've got some catching up to do."

"No, I wanna get back," he said.

"How about if we come back next week and take you out for your birthday and Father's Day," said my husband. "We can catch up then."

"Sure," said Dad. "That's fine."

"Do you want a ride to your place?" asked my husband.

"No, I'll walk," Dad said.

"All right, then," I said, emotionally and physically exhausted. "I want to go home."

Tommy, Dad, Charlie and I eating dinner al fresco
Sorrento, Italy, 1959

———————•◄——————

CHAPTER TWENTY-FIVE

The Warehouse

Dad's birthday always fell near, if not on, Father's Day, and was exactly one week before mine. We usually combined the three occasions in one celebration, a fact he often noted bitterly. His fifty-seventh birthday landed on Saturday, June 16, 1979. My baby was due July 8. It was a clear, warm summer night as my husband and I found our way to the warehouse. Dad had left the chain-link gate ajar for us. Inside the fence, four rows of windowless rectangular buildings were centered in an area about an acre square surrounded by gray asphalt. It could have been a concentration camp.

Driving around two of the structures, we found Dad watering a small cluster of palms potted in wine barrels that created a small oasis outside the door of the caretaker's unit attached to one of the warehouse buildings. He greeted us in surprisingly good spirits. His hair was still wet and curly from taking a shower. He smelled good, of Old Spice, and his blue jeans were clean as was his Oxford shirt, though still unpressed and missing a couple of buttons.

"Let me give you the fifty-cent tour of my villa," he said as soon as my foot peeked out of the door on the passenger side. As I started to walk, I saw Maria, Tomoso e Carlo, the original frieze of the three cupid's faces he'd purchased in Italy and copied in Ventura, hanging on the wall by the door to his apartment. Urns, junk sculptures and the palms created a circle around a seating area of chipped and rusty patio furniture. A plaster table embedded with an amateurish mosaic of shells, driftwood and sea glass held a tray with crackers and cheese, three wine glasses, and a bottle of Lancer's rosé.

It only took a minute to see his apartment, which consisted of one room and a bathroom, a far cry from his apartment in Chicago or the Big House. There was no area for cooking and the twin bed looked awfully small. As far back as I could remember, Dad and whatever books and newspapers he was reading had filled a king-sized bed.

The asphalt had been hosed down before we arrived giving it the smell of a red-tiled Italian patio in Sorrento after a rain. Walking from plant to plant Dad said, "Walter and Eloise, who are letting me use this place, helped me haul the raphis palms with their pick-up. The plants don't like being in the sun this much, but I think they'll acclimate eventually. They may not stay as green. I've gathered the outdoor furniture from various and sundry yard sales around. There's lots of space here for entertaining, as you can see. Several functional seating areas."

I thought to myself, "I bet we are the only guests he's ever had here." As far as I'd been aware of, during the time he lived on Chautauqua, Dad had received only one set of visitors besides his children, his younger brother Bobby's family when they flew out from Maryland to see him. I'd never seen Dad talk on the phone and I'd never heard it ring. The only conversations he'd reported were those he'd had with the waitresses and customers at Norm's Coffee Shop.

"I thought we'd have a little al fresco cocktail party before we head to dinner," Dad said, ushering us to the area where the wine and cheese were waiting. I sat in the lawn chair, trying carefully not to catch my stockings on the dangling metal pieces sticking out of the bottom of the chair. Once we were settled, however, we were quite comfortable and enjoyed the balmy air.

We arrived at the Belle Vue on time for our seven-o'clock reservation. I caught a trace of disappointment when Dad glanced around the room in search of movie stars. We sat in a spacious semi-circle booth with me in the middle and Dad on my left. I waited until we ordered before asking him about his disappearance.

"Within a week of receiving my foreclosure notice from the bank that held my mortgage, this S.O.B. Harris sends some guy around saying I had to leave or be carried out. I moved into the Falcon," he said.

Until the week before, Dad's car lay like a dead whale at the farthest corner of his parking lot. It was missing a wheel and the rest of the tires were flat. It still had its windows, but the fenders and doors were badly dented and rusty. I had no idea if there was an engine under the hood.

"Then that damned developer Harris went and called the police who showed up the next morning while I was still dead asleep and yanked me by the arm out of the car. I hit my glasses against the door of the car and they jabbed me right in the eye. Amidst the pain I was feeling, I was trying to explain to the officer that my car was actually on city property, not the property of my apartment house, so Harris had no right to do anything about my being there. But the officer wouldn't listen to me. He just stuffed me into his patrol car and hauled me off to the city jail.

"At the jailhouse, they realized my eye was hurt and sent me in an ambulance to the Veterans' Hospital in Westwood. I figured that while I was in there getting treated for my eye, I might as well get those cancer spots on my back removed. But while I was checked in there, Harris pulled a fast one and contacted you.

"Meanwhile, there is this other guy, Richardson, who knew my building was in foreclosure and tried to bid on the place, but wasn't allowed into the bidding. He has filed a lawsuit against the bank for unlawfully giving Harris the property for the pitiful sum of a million dollars. Why, that place is worth five million, easy. There should have been a public auction or something to get the highest bidder, but that Harris guy was in bed with the bank and didn't have to bid against anyone."

Dad put his thumb and index fingers into his breast pocket and pulled out a dog-eared envelope folded in thirds. He tore the corner off the envelope where the return address was printed and handed it to me. "That's the name of the law firm representing me." he said proudly. I read the name quickly: Reezer and Associates. What caught my eye was the Century City address. It wasn't clear to me how Dad had enough presence of mind or money to hire an apparently expensive and established law firm.

"Just keep that," he said.

The rest of dinner went relatively smoothly. He had little alcohol to drink and his mood remained stable as he finished his pork chops and we talked about getting ready for the birth of his first grandchild who'd spent the dinner kicking me in the ribs. As we left the restaurant, we asked Dad where he wanted us to take him. "Just drop me off at my building. It's my birthday. I want to watch the sunset from my corner."

In my last image of my father, I can still see him sitting on the street curb in front of the Chautauqua apartment building. I watched him through the rear window of our '68 VW bus as he waved farewell to me, while my husband drove down Pacific Coast Highway towards our home in Pasadena. I returned his wave with the same rhythm, like a windshield wiper. His jean-covered rump was perched on the edge of the curb. His feet were planted flat on the pavement. The traffic on PCH was whizzing past him. He was smiling.

My belief in a better day had been revived. Thinking about it now and knowing what happened next, it was probably the last time I trusted that feeling.

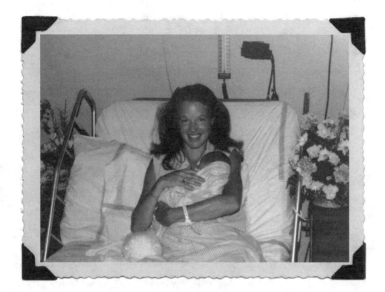

With baby Jonathan, July 17, 1979

———◆———

CHAPTER TWENTY-SIX

Good-Bye

During the time between Dad's birthday celebration and the birth of my son three weeks later, Mr. Rathberg must have shown Dad the letter I'd signed to obtain the release of the family furniture. Or maybe he told my father something that was not true. Or maybe my father didn't read the document carefully and jumped to the wrong conclusion. All I know is that by the time I had delivered his first grandchild, my father believed I had betrayed him and joined the forces of evil who had taken away his apartment building. The result was that he told my husband, "If she wants to talk to me, she has to go through his attorney."

After my husband relayed this message to me in the hospital, I recalled the corner piece of envelope with the address Dad had given me at the Belle Vue and tried to remember where I'd put it. But by the time I got home with my new little bundle, I was so busy learning how to change diapers I forgot about it again.

For the next few months, I assumed Dad would realize he'd misunderstood and give me a call. But as Jonathan grew, turned one and I became pregnant with a second child, I heard nothing. I knew Dad wouldn't admit he'd made a mistake, but I thought he'd eventually ignore the incident so he could see his grandchild. Even if he didn't want to see me, at the very least I assumed he'd want to fetch his precious belongings.

The furniture and boxes were still piled three layers deep in our garage, collecting dust and spider webs. The plants, which God created to live in a moist and shady tropical setting, were not happy outdoors in dry Pasadena. The shade cover we'd built barely kept the leaves of the palms from burning. It took me several hours every few days to water the pots while Jonathan looked over my shoulder from a pack strapped to my aching back. As I watched the water fill each planter, I noticed the bare roots. The plants needed replanting and fertilizing, neither of which I had the time, money or strength to do. Instead I muttered bitterly, "Dad, get over here and take care of your own stupid plants."

On May 26 two years later, I gave birth to my daughter Amy. For the announcement, I drew a picture of Jonathan as a toddler pulling a HiFlyer wagon with his new baby sister sitting in it. I printed the announcement for my family and friends on pink card stock and mailed them in pink envelopes. I addressed one of the cards to Dad at the warehouse address. It would have arrived the first week of June, but the following week it was returned to me. The postman delivered the unopened pink envelope back in my mailbox with Dad's handwriting all over the front, "Return to sender. Guilt card unnecessary."

In spite of the pink color, I suspected that Dad mistakenly thought the card was for his birthday and Father's Day. Even with my resolve not to care, I couldn't block out my distress. I wouldn't believe he didn't want to know he had a granddaughter.

Another year went by, during which my husband and I were

divorced. I remained in the house where we'd lived and a few months after my husband moved out I received a phone call from a young attorney who said he worked for Reezer and Associates. He told me, "Our firm was hired by your father to defend him in his case against Harris Development for wrongful possession of his property. The court date is coming up in a few weeks and we can't find your father anywhere. We drove to the address we had for him. It turned out to be an old warehouse, which has burned down. I hate to bother you, but your father did give us your name and we wondered if you might be able to help us find him."

I pictured my father burning in his apartment, the semi-circle of potted plants leaving a charred skeleton like those left after fires in the nearby Angeles National Forest caused by a stray cigarette.

"Is he alive?" I asked.

"Yes ma'am. He'd moved out, but no one seems to know where he went."

Feeling partial relief, I said, "Have you tried to find him at Norm's Coffee Shop in Santa Monica? There's a good chance he'll show up there between four and six in the morning."

"I'll try that," he said. "Also, we understand you and your husband were approached by the development firm. Will the two of you be willing to testify in the case?"

"Sir, I think once you have talked to my father you will find he doesn't want me to have anything to do with him or this case."

As I hung up the phone I wondered why Dad spent so much time and energy on his legal case and neglected to tell the lawyers where he was. How was he keeping alive? Where was he sleeping at night? How was he eating? Would he ever give up?

The garage at the foot of my property in Pasadena

CHAPTER TWENTY-SEVEN

The Flood

Several more months went by before the young man at Reezer and Associates called me back. "I just want you to know I found your father at Norm's Coffee Shop," he said. "He subsequently met with us in our office. You were right. He didn't want you to testify in the case, but I thought you'd like to know he asked about you. He was interested to know you had a second child and I also told him about your divorce."

This spark of news melted my resolve not to need a father just a little. "If Dad is that interested in my affairs," I thought, "I'm sure he'll contact me eventually."

Another year went by before a different associate from the same law firm called me. "We won your father's case for him," he announced. "We also won a fairly large monetary award for him, but he's disappeared again and we were hoping he might have contacted you."

I didn't know if the associate was too lazy to get up early enough to catch Dad at Norm's or Dad was avoiding him. I suggested he try again. He never called back and I never learned the results of the search. That was the last contact I had from Reezer and Associates, but I worried less about my father, because I knew he had some money.

Two more years went by. Still no word from Dad. Instead I was visited by a winter of torrential rains. My garage, at the back of my property, was downhill from my house. After several weeks of downpour I found four inches of water covering the bases of Dad's furniture and the bottoms of boxes resting on the garage floor. It was several more days before it stopped raining enough and I had gathered enough neighborhood muscle to pull everything out of the garage for an inspection.

Many items were permanently damaged. The clubfeet on the highboy and my great-grandfather's Federal desk were swollen and discolored. A box that turned out to contain old photographs of Dad's ancestors was soaked through. I tried to separate the photos, but some of them had fused like one piece of soggy cardboard, century-old images stuck face to face forever. Many of those that survived were moldy and faded and the handwritten labels on the backs were smeared beyond legibility.

A box containing my collection of foreign dolls was trapped under all of Dad's boxes. Being at the bottom, it received the worst damage from the water. There were dolls from Egypt, Thailand, China, Japan and the other countries my Grandfather Hopkins had visited which he gave me when he returned from his yearly world tours. There were also dolls from Scotland, England, Italy, Russia, Belgium, Switzerland, Holland, France and Alaska I'd added from my own travels. I spent hours as a little girl rearranging the dolls in a glass cabinet in my bedroom. In my grown-up house with children there wasn't enough room for them, so I'd carefully packed them away in the garage before the great furniture rescue.

When I opened the box to find the faces distorted with mildew pockmarks and the beautiful costumes rotted and brown, I started weeping.

I was angry with my father for leaving me with all his junk to take care of. I still viewed him as if I were a child, denying to myself he was mentally ill. It would be a few more years before I could face it. It wasn't his fault my house had been flooded, but from that moment on, I stopped saving things for him in my garage. I stopped thinking he was going to come back and fetch his belongings and I tried to stop hoping he wanted to see me again.

I moved the antique furniture into my home. The highboy went into my bedroom where I needed a dresser. The Federal desk and the gate-leg table fit in the living room. I got rid of the junk from other people's apartments in a series of yard sales. Everything was filthy from spending five years in my uninsulated garage. I spent several hours with gobs of furniture polish and piles of old rags cleaning the Federal desk, trying to cover the scratches and yellowed claw feet with dark brown wood stain.

Not until I was swiping the spider webs from underneath the gate-leg table did I realize the drawer with the old appraisal stuck inside was missing. I knew intuitively it wasn't lost and that Dad had taken it with him to the warehouse. I could picture him walking away from the rest of his stuff at Chautauqua, the drawer tucked under his arm like a large newspaper. He would cherish that drawer as I did my old love letters in a box under my bed.

If that drawer had been equipped with a tracking device, I could have found my father a lot sooner than I did.

Dad and his aunt Rosemary in Sante Fe, New Mexico, 1962

————◆————

CHAPTER TWENTY-EIGHT

Family Connections

In 1990 I married a man who lived and worked in San Francisco. I'd received no new address for Dad since the burning of the warehouse and I didn't feel like sending my moving announcement and wedding invitation to Thomas Ames c/o Norm's Coffee Shop. Also, I was afraid he would send it back.

A few months before I moved, I'd seen an advertisement for a mental health hotline on a bus-stop billboard and jotted down the number. Once home I called to ask if there was something I should be doing to help my father. When I'd explained the situation to the woman at the other end of the hotline she said, "Do you know if he is in danger?"

"No, I don't."

"Do you know if he's hurting anyone?"

"No, I don't know that, either, but I doubt it."

"As long as he isn't in any danger to himself or to someone else, then you owe it to him to follow his request and leave him alone," she said.

I must have wanted to believe she was right, because I followed her advice until a few months later when I went to a party with some friends and met a Pasadena police officer. I mentioned casually that I'd lost track of my father and was curious to know how one would go about finding someone like that.

"I could look him up on the computer," she said.

She called me the next day. "I was able to find out that your dad applied for a Senior Citizens Identification Card a few months ago, but that's about all the information I can legally give you. Basically this means he isn't driving anymore and needed some sort of identification."

It meant a lot to me. He was still alive and he was still being resourceful. I briefly considered driving to Norm's one morning to see if he showed up. Then I tried to imagine what I would say to him once I saw him, but I couldn't, so I decided not to go. I was practicing avoidance on the highest level. Now that I was living in San Francisco, Dad couldn't find me either. It had been eleven years since I'd seen him. I'd spent the last five of those attending art school to obtain a fine arts' degree in graphics and packaging, juggling homework with carpooling and leading my daughter's third grade Brownie troop.

Dad missed another graduation, but I knew he would have been proud of me. "You should be a graphic designer," he said every year when I gave him my latest Christmas card. I'd learned a few printing techniques at Wheaton. In my senior year I carved a peace dove out of a linoleum block and hand pressed about fifty copies for friends and family. Dad took the one I'd sent him and pasted it onto the upper-left-hand corner of a piece of typing paper. In the right corner opposite he typed "Ames Graphics" and my address. Then he xeroxed some thirty copies of this new letterhead for me and gave it to me as a birthday present. "Here you go.

Now you are officially in business," he said.

I hoped my move to San Francisco would allow me a fresh start with a man who was on my side. My feelings about my father were in a state of limbo. My new husband had never met him, but promised to be supportive of me. I deluded myself into thinking that if I left Pasadena, I could leave my confused feelings behind. Actually, all I did was make everything I needed to deal with harder to get to.

A few months later, my Uncle Bobby in Hagerstown, Maryland called to invite my children, new husband and me to an Ames Reunion in August. The clan should have consisted of three families: his, Uncle Bud's, and my father's. However, Uncle Bud's family didn't make it. We ended up with twenty-one for dinner each night for a week. Since I seldom saw my own brothers, and I never saw them without our mother present, it was the first chance we had to sit and talk about our disappearing father in any depth. During golf games, by the pool having cocktails, eating hot dogs at the local baseball game, we compared notes with each other and our uncle.

"Did Dad say good-bye to either of you?" I asked my brothers.

"I sent him a couple of letters after he told you to stop talking to him," said Tommy. "He never wrote back. When I heard he'd returned your baby announcement for Amy unopened, I thought, 'What's the point?' I suppose we could go down to that coffee shop where he used to hang out and see what's up. I just don't think he wants to see us."

"I remember that night when the warehouse burned down," said Paula, my younger brother Charlie's wife. "It was back when Charles and I were students, still dating. Charles came to my apartment one night unexpectedly and pounded on the door. When I opened it, he looked terribly depressed and said, 'We don't know where my dad is. We thought he was living in this warehouse and my sister just called to say it has burned down. Now we don't know where he's gone.'"

"I tried calling your father about the same time," said Uncle Bobby. "He said the same thing to me, 'If you want to talk to me, call my attorney,' which was followed by the sound of a phone replaced heavily in its cradle."

Bobby's daughter, my twenty-two-year-old cousin Haven, said, "I'll never forget that time Mom and Dad took me to see Uncle Tommy in California. It must have been in 1976, because I was eight and was so excited to be visiting my eccentric uncle living on a beach in L.A. Uncle Tommy must have known of his reputation, because he got dressed up in costume to meet us at the airport. When I walked off the plane, there he was with this huge mischievous smile, dressed like a hippie. He had on bell-bottomed jeans full of holes and a bright tie-dyed tee shirt. He wore a long-haired wig that he must have got from a thrift store and a beaded headband that crossed his forehead like an Indian headdress with droplets of beads hanging down in front of his face, which was all tan and leathery. I loved it and he knew I would. It made him so happy to get a laugh out of me."

It was comforting to know we shared similar emotions. We all missed the man Dad used to be and were hurt that the man he had become wanted to exclude us from his life. But no one dared venture any theories of why he had done so or said, "He just doesn't love us any more and wants to be away from us," because we didn't think that was the case. On the other hand, we didn't say, "Tom Ames has gone crazy. He needs help and we don't know how to help him."

Were we all in denial or so weak we didn't want to take on the responsibility? Or did we simply believe that, even though he was angry and somewhat crazy, he was perfectly capable of taking care of himself and wanted to be left alone?

There was a reserved tone in the conversations, as though we were afraid Dad knew his family was getting together without him and could overhear us. The man we remembered wouldn't have liked being left out of a party and he wouldn't have liked our talking about him when he wasn't there. It was as if we were at a funeral for a person who hadn't died.

There was also something eerie that my brothers and I shared during that visit. Uncle Bobby's mannerisms and voice were so like our father's we felt as if we had our dad back in some way. During the week, the three of us each experienced hearing our uncle's voice in another room and thinking it was our father for a moment. Just the sound of his voice made us realize we missed something we'd forgotten about. "We really love you kids," Aunt Kay kept repeating. "Don't think that just because your dad isn't talking to us we aren't still here for you." It felt good to hear that.

———————

A few months later I received a letter from another Ames relative, Dad's cousin Julie whom I hadn't yet met, though I'd known of her existence. I had corresponded with her mother, Dad's Aunt Rosemary, since my family visited her in Sante Fe in 1962. Without knowing her relationship to me, Julie wrote to tell me Rosemary had died because she had found copies of my letters among her mother's possessions and "thought I might want to know."

When we were growing up, Dad kept a picture on our piano of Rosemary holding the hand of five-year-old Shirley Temple standing with the rest of the cast of *Our Little Girl*. One day I asked if Rosemary ever had any children. She was famous in our house for having been married four times as well as for being an actress. "She had a little girl named Julie with her first husband who must be about eight or ten years younger than I." Dad said, and then explained how Rosemary moved to Hollywood without Julie. At the time, I imagined her as a poor little waif abandoned by her mother, floating around the world somewhere.

From the return address on Julie's letter I realized she lived in Tiburon, across the bay from my home in San Francisco. I found her number in the directory and gave her a call. At sixty-two, Julie was no waif, though she is tiny. When I explained my connection, she said, "Oh, I know who you are," in a spunky voice. "Your dad and I spent the summer of 1941 together at our grandmother's house on Shelter Island, right before the bombing of Pearl Harbor. I was thirteen and your dad was eighteen. How is he?"

I gave her the latest information.

"Well, you know your dad is gay, don't you?"

I felt like I'd been shot with a stun gun. I knew Dad had mannerisms some might call "swishy," but this pronouncement from a cousin whom I'd yet to meet was as much of a shock as it would have been if she'd told me I was adopted.

"What makes you say that?" I squeaked out.

The tone of her voice changed when she realized she'd caught me off guard. "He used to act really girlish," she said simply. "All I'm trying to say is that the reason he might have wanted to withdraw from his family was because he wanted to live his own life-style, without having to account to his children."

"Well, um, I hadn't considered that before." I said, changing the topic of the conversation to her mother.

Rosemary had been living in Mystic, Connecticut. Her letters to me had indicated she was terrified of getting old and had claimed for twenty years she was in her late sixties. She'd spent her entire life after Hollywood researching ancestors of the Ames family, tramping through New England's graveyards, and sifting through birth, marriage and death records in churches and city-hall libraries. She believed if we understood our ancestors, we would understand ourselves and had sent reams of copies of her records to me. She often wrote, "Be sure you ask me any questions you have about our family, Mary, because I won't be around forever." Unfortunately, I didn't get around to reading all the manuscripts until I went to write this story.

Like our Puritan ancestors, Rosemary had remained very independent and loved her garden. At age "sixty-nine" she wrote, "I pulled out two tree stumps this weekend and made jam from all the plums from the tree outside my kitchen window." However, like her brother, the Mystery Man, and her father Snake, she'd lost, or had never found, the Puritan's faith in God and the belief that we are here on earth to serve Him.

She planned her suicide very carefully, maybe because she remembered the mess her father had made. She distributed to family members what she thought were her important belongings. Then she neatly labeled everything left in her house so Julie wouldn't be bothered too much taking care of it and wrote instructions about what to do with her body in a letter addressed to Julie's thirty-year-old son Adam. After swallowing a bottle-full of sleeping pills, she went to her car in the garage, sat there and waited. The following day the letter reached Adam in Florida who called his mother in Tiburon. Then she and her husband flew back to Connecticut to find Rosemary in her garage.

This was the third, if not fourth, of dad's immediate family to take their own life. I hoped he wouldn't find out about it.

Julie and I set a date to get together for lunch before I hung up the phone. I stayed on the stool in front of my drafting table staring out the window across the bay towards Tiburon, feeling sorry for Rosemary and Julie and dazed by what she'd told me about my father.

I reviewed my memories of him in light of what I'd observed about gay men and realized he never talked about his pursuits and conquests of women, nor had he dated that I knew of since divorcing my mother. He was an overly sensitive man, highly emotional, and kept his body in good shape by lifting weights regularly and wore clothing which showed off his physique.

All these things could have been quite normal for a hetero-sexual male, yet I thought about how uncomfortable I used to be when he wore that tiny Italian bikini on the beach in Ventura. Though I considered my father's mannerisms weird as a child, it never dawned on me he might be gay. The popularity of *coming out* was new in my world. Homosexuality wasn't even a word in my vocabulary until I was in college. The change in awareness of homosexuality between 1960 Pasadena and 1990 San Francisco was enormous.

I immediately called my mother who said, "We only had as much of a sex life as it took to conceive the three of you." The amazing thing was that she said it with such an air of relief as if she'd been wanting to let me know that for a very long time.

"Did he come out? Did he have gay relationships?" I asked.

"No, not that I knew of," she said. "But the architect who rented an office from us at your father's store said your father would hit on the young associates working in their studio. He also said he saw your dad in Laguna Beach one weekend hanging out with a gay crowd. But that is just hearsay, I suppose."

"Mom," I yelled into the phone, "do you think Dad is gay?"

"Don't shout, dear. Yes, I do."

Next I called my Uncle Bobby. At first he was upset by what he considered an accusation. Then he said, "Well, our father used to call him a sissy. Tommy may not be particularly sexual, but though he is the most emotional of the three of us, he isn't gay."

In the '20s when Dad was born, it was a crime in many places to be a homosexual. If you were caught in a homosexual act, you could spend up to twenty years in prison. Gayness was considered an unnatural state of being. The new hypno-therapists of the day tried to help gay men talk themselves out of their desires for men and into desiring women. The attractions felt by a homosexual person were unacceptable. If the subject was brought up in fine society, it was quickly ignored or dismissed.

Dad considered himself high society. His father and grandfather, with whom he'd lived the first eleven years of his life, were college football stars and powerful businessmen. If Dad was a homosexual, it wouldn't be surprising he would want to hide it from them. "I don't think your father wanted to be gay," Mom told me. "That's why he was in such a hurry to get married and have children." Was it possible that he felt so bad about it that it was a secret he meant to keep forever?

Dad in the army, around 1943

CHAPTER TWENTY-NINE

The War Years

Among the papers I'd rescued from Chautauqua was a packet of letters written from my uncles, Bobby and Bud, to my father during World War II and a collection of letters from other friends and family he'd received during the same period.

The parents of all children growing up in the '50s were involved in World War II in some way. My father was in the army. My friend Christine's father was a navy man. The fellow next door was a scientist who'd worked at Caltech's Jet Propulsion Laboratory nearby, developing bombs and the aircraft that carried them. The movies in those days that weren't Westerns were about war heroes or war-time romances. Kids would brag about what their fathers did during the war, so one day when I was ten, I asked my father specifically what he had done in the army.

"I shuffled papers," he said.

"What do you mean, you shuffled papers?"

"I took them out of one pile and put them in another."

"Why did you do that?"

"You'll understand when you get older," he said. All I'd learned was that the conversation was over.

Reboxing the letters I'd salvaged after the flood in my garage, I stopped to read the letters Bud and Bobby had written. Later I filled in some of the gaps in the story by calling my uncles on the phone.

When the U.S. entered the war in December of '41, Dad was a sophomore at PJC, Bobby a senior at South Pasadena High School and Bud a senior at Stanford. Only Bud was eligible for service and when he walked through the door of his mother's and stepfather's house in San Marino for his Christmas vacation three weeks after Pearl Harbor, his orders from the War Department were in his mother's hand.

Bud told me, "This'll show you the sadistic nature of your father's jokes. On the outside of the cable was printed 'SAN FRANCISCO PORT OF EMBARKATION,' and when Mother saw the cable, she panicked. 'They can't ship you,' she said. 'You have no training!'

"Whereupon your father said, 'Mom, it actually makes a great deal of sense. They're losing a lot of troopships between Honolulu and San Francisco. They're all getting sunk. So they're shipping Bud first and if he makes it across the ocean, then it'll be worth training him.'"

The War Department allowed Bud to finish college before sending him to training. Then he was shipped to Cairo. His four years at Shattuck Military Academy enabled him to enter the army as an officer, but he was never on the firing line. Instead he spent the entire war doing something his father and grandfather had done, publishing a newspaper. The army's weekly paper was called *YANK*. First Bud worked in Cairo, then in the Pacific.

Dad was eligible for the draft soon after Bud entered the war.

"I rescued your father from the firing line by talking the army into admitting him into the Army Special Training Program taught at Stanford, called the ASTP," he said.

My mother told me a different reason Dad spent the entire four years stateside. She said it was because his eyesight was so poor. After graduating from the training program, Dad worked in the psychology department at Sheppard Field in Texas testing soldiers who were about to go overseas, either as spies or officers. From Texas he moved to Atlantic City, then Orlando, Florida, and finally Kentucky. A letter from his cousin Julie to him in Kentucky indicated he'd given her another phony reason for the stateside postings, "Your overseas excuse has changed I see. Last time it was flat feet instead of high arches. You must have done the exercises over-strenuously."

Bobby wrote in one letter, "My God, Ferry Boy, do you ever stay at your base? Every time I get a letter from you, you are coming from, or just going to some city." Later he wrote, "I've finally figured out what your job is from your letters. On the 15th of the month you sign the payroll and on the month-end you collect."

Bud wrote, "Your letters get better and better, and I might add, wetter and wetter, since I seem to find a dry martini in every other line. Doesn't look like you're having too rough a time. And judging by your schedule in the last letter, you still are a question mark to the people you work for. Can't anybody find where you fit?"

Bobby was sent to Foggia, Italy, by the air force. During the course of two years, he flew over fifty missions in B-17 bombers, fighting a war he has never wanted to talk about.

As the only brother stateside, Dad was the source of goodies. Bud's letters consistently requested cigarettes. "Things got so pinched that today I went to the PX and bought two sacks of Bull

Durham, which is not rationed. Now I'm trying to roll my own. There's tobacco flakes from here to Alexandria."

Bobby's letters reminded me of those my son wrote me from summer camp and boarding school. He wanted food. "How about running to a grocery store some day and picking up some unrationed food stuffs for your poor, half-starved younger brother? Powdered soup, spreads, sardines, etc."

In a later letter he wrote, "I got your box of food the other night. Another package from you came last night and I'm fascinated with the spaghetti dinner that was included." I guess he wondered why Dad sent spaghetti to a brother in Italy.

In the same package as the letters from his brothers were two tiny photographs of a man standing at the side of a railroad track, labeled on the back, KLA, Jr. Miami, 31 Jan 45 in Dad's handwriting (KLA being the initials for Knowlton Lyman Ames, aka Dad's father, Juny and the Mystery Man). The photos were almost identical except that in one, he had his hat on and in the other he did not.

Juny had been contributing his efforts to the war also, managing the Prince George Hotel in Nassau. One news clipping said, "He served, without compensation, as Welfare Officer to the Royal Air Force based there." When I asked Uncle Bud about this article, he translated it as follows.

"During World War II, officers in England sent their brides to the Bahamas to get them away from the blitzkrieg. Our dad got hold of one of these brides and made a baby sister for my brothers and me. The husband of this bride found out about it, but he forgave his wife and took both his bride and the little girl back to England. I never met my sister or learned her name. But this didn't slow down our father's social schedule. He was soon pursuing a former British show girl named Olivia Travers, who eventually become wife Number Three."

In Rosemary's manuscript, she wrote, "Juny attracted and was friendly towards all classes of people and entertained America's best-known personalities at his home in Nassau. He entertained people as varied as the Duke and Duchess of Windsor to Errol Flynn and American celebrities."

Juny often took these guests deep-sea fishing, a serious sport for him. Bud told me, "One day our father caught a magnificent wahoo. Realizing it was an exceptionally large fish, he immediately had it frozen because the only scale big enough to measure it was way up in Florida and he would have to deliver it in his boat. It turned out his efforts were worth it, for his fish broke a world record, which he held for over thirty years."

While my dad was stationed in Florida, he decided to visit his father, but this turned out to be a very bad idea. "The old man was much more interested in fishing and chasing women than in being a father," Uncle Bobby told me. "And Olivia was closer in age to your dad than she was to our father. She was very beautiful, though. Her hair was as red as an Irish setter's. *Life* magazine published a photo of her sitting at the old man's bar at the Prince George Hotel. While your dad was in Nassau, he was virtually put in the closet. Our father didn't want Olivia knowing he had such an old son."

The tiny photos of KLA, Jr. were taken by Dad when he left his father, who must have accompanied him back as far as Miami. "Whenever your father talked about that last visit," said Mom, "it was with a great deal of bitterness. He was never to visit his father again and his father was never to visit him. It was from that point on that he became the Mystery Man."

In the box which held the packet of war letters from Bud and Bobby were more letters and newspaper clippings, including a photo of a beautiful woman I did not recognize. It led me to the story of the only serious tragedy Dad experienced during the war firsthand. The young woman was in her late teens or early twenties. The print was cropped at her shoulders. Her dark hair was pulled gently back behind her head and she wore a suit of tiny checkers with a great big bow at her neck. She seemed very demure and proper. The photo wasn't posed, for though her face was square with the camera, her large dark eyes were looking unsurely to her left as if someone had just called her name. She had a nice smile, showing perfect teeth.

Curiosity piqued, I showed the photo to my mother and asked, "Do you know who this woman is?"

"No, I have no idea. But I do know that your father asked two women to marry him before he asked me and they both said no."

The woman's identity became clear after more paper-shuffling. In the packet of letters from my uncles was a white envelope with a matching letter in it, addressed in a feminine hand. The return address engraved in black block letters caught my attention, for it said, "CLARE BOOTHE LUCE, HOUSE OF REPRESENTATIVES, WASHINGTON, D.C." It was stamped with the postmark March 4, 1944 and addressed to "Private Tom Ames, Psychology Section, Sheppard Field, Texas," Dad's first post. I pulled out the singly folded letter engraved in the same manner and read this note.

Dear Tom Ames,

I was deeply touched by your letter, and the beautiful flowers you sent to the chapel at Stanford. I see you were very fond of my child, and she, so she told me often, liked you enormously. She was gay and happy whenever she mentioned your name, and I expect that meant that she had a happy and gay time when she was with you. So I am grateful to you for this: that you made moments of her life her short life—happy moments. I shall keep that fact always in warm remembrance.

Time passes. I do not seem to grieve one bit less for my child. In fact, the loss becomes more incredible and more wounding every day, for every day I realize more and more how she was all the wealth of my heart, and all that I meant by my "hopes for the future."

And yet, it must be lived with and endured, this sorrow. And made even, fruitful. That's the only way gay and lovely and sharing Ann would have it.

Bless you. Take care. All best luck. Cordially
—Claire Boothe Luce.

I felt like a sleuth trying to figure out the mystery of the missing ruby. As I dug deeper I came across four letters and a telegram also addressed to Dad at Sheppard Field, but this time the postmark read Stanford University. Two of them were engraved with Ann Clare Brokaw's Kappa House address. "Maybe this is the Ann that Mrs. Luce was talking about," I thought. They were all sent the year before, 1943.

The earliest, the telegram, was postmarked October 7 and read:

STANFORD UNIVERSITY CALIF
CHUG CHUG HERE I COME
DELIGHTED WITH YOUR PLAN
ANN.
CHUG CHUG.

Dad must have met Ann when he was in the ASTP program at

Stanford. I was thankful he'd kept her letters in their envelopes, for it helped with my detective work, but there was no further reference to this proposed trip. The next message was dated November 23 in which Ann wrote about her social life at Stanford and about a car accident one of her good friends had been in. "Poor thing – I know she feels wretched & her car which was just sent up from L.A. a week ago is – of course – a wreck."

In the next letter, dated fourteen days later on December 7, she described more of her sorority life. The last, written on notebook paper with three holes punched, was sent December 29, right after Christmas. Ann thanked Dad for some records, a Gilbert & Sullivan book and the "blissful book-plates" he'd sent to her.

> *Exams are going full tilt. Two more to go ('Personality Integration East & West' – psychology, in case that should interest you – and "International Law') then whee – down to Palm Springs with the [S]ales to meet my Ma & Pa! Must tear now – so 'scuse the scrawl & paper and all.*
> *—Ann*
> *Tct tct. Don't I sound collegiate?*

The answer to the puzzle was in the form of two newspaper articles. The first one identified the woman. She was sitting next to another pretty lady on a couch beneath a headline which read, "Rep. Clare Boothe Luce Sees Women Taking Leading Role in Postwar Politics." The caption under the photo identified Clare with her daughter Ann Brokaw.

The photo in the second news article was the same photo that I had found in the packet of letters, except for one thing. The photo in the article was complete, for sitting next to Ann, in the direction where she was looking, was her mother. In Dad's copy of the photo Clare was cropped out. Strangely enough, Dad's photo wasn't xeroxed from the news article, for it was much clearer. Maybe he asked the paper for an original print. The headline read, "Daughter of Rep. Luce Killed in Auto Crash," and the caption explained, "Ann Clare Brokaw, at right, daughter of Clare Boothe Luce, at left, was killed in auto accident at Palo Alto, Cal., yesterday. She was returning to Stanford after visiting mother in San Francisco where this picture was made."

In the thirteen days between December 29, 1943, when Dad received his last letter from Ann, and January 11, 1944, when she was killed, Ann Clare Brokaw visited her mother and stepfather in Palm Springs, returned with her mother to San Francisco for the speech and then returned to Palo Alto for school. The article described the accident.

"PALO ALTO, Jan. 11 [1944]. (U.P.) – Ann Claire Brokaw, 19, only daughter of Rep. Claire Boothe Luce (R.) Ct. was killed in an automobile collision here today while she was riding with a friend to her classes at Stanford University. She had accompanied her mother from Los Angeles to San Francisco yesterday. … As they entered an intersection, a car collided with the Hobbs car, police reported. The Hobbs' car spun around and the front door flew open. Miss Brokaw was hurled out, striking a tree. She was crushed between the car and the tree and apparently died immediately … Miss Brokaw was the daughter of Rep. Luce by her first marriage, with the late George T. Brokaw, heir to the Isaac Vail Brokaw clothing fortune."

A little research filled in the picture: At the time Clare wrote the thank-you letter to Dad, she was a member of the House of

Representatives for the United States and was a well-known play-wright having written *The Women*, the most attended Broadway show in history at the time. In 1939 it was made into a movie. Clare had first married George T. Brokaw, an abusive alcoholic. That marriage ended in divorce and in 1933 she married Henry Luce, publisher of *Time* and *Life* magazines.

While Clare was busy being who she was, Ann was sent away to schools or taken care of by nannies. Her relationship with her father had not been any closer. She grew up to be an insecure young lady, often sullen and unhappy. It's easy to imagine Dad's relating to her. He was also attracted to people in the spotlight.

Dad sent flowers to Clare Boothe Luce at least two more times, for there were two more corresponding thank-you letters, one on the anniversary of Ann's death in 1945, another in 1946.

I called Bud to ask him what he knew, "Never heard of her."

"I didn't know a thing about it," added Bobby.

Dad must have been harboring thoughts about Ann for a long time for I noticed it was in 1975, ten years after his divorce from my mother, that the original photo I found in a photohouse envelope was printed from its negative. The address given on the envelope for the client was Dad's Santa Monica apartment building, revealing he had copies made of Ann's photo more than thirty years after her death.

After Ann's death her mother became a Catholic and donated money to the chapel in Palo Alto mentioned in the note to Dad; it was named St. Ann's in honor of her daughter. When Clare died of a brain tumor in 1987, the importance of the memorial was nearly forgotten. Then on February 26, 1999, the *San Francisco Chronicle* reported that the Roman Catholic diocese of San Jose wanted to sell the chapel to developers to raise funds, but the parishioners and city council of Palo Alto wanted to raise money to save it. The

Luce Foundation stepped in to help the parishioners. Eventually the Episcopal church to which I belonged purchased the chapel and for now it is being used as it was intended, though – as with the statue of my ancestor Lieutenant Colonel Knowlton – few who pass the chapel know the story behind it.

The last dated letter in the packet was from Dad's brother Bud, written when the war came to an end. He discussed their future prospects upon their release from service. Bud had enjoyed working on *YANK* so much he wanted to continue in the publishing business when the war was over. Hoping Dad would join the venture, he sent him a detailed business plan. "I know Nanna is interested in some of my future plans. How you will fit into the picture will be up to you. I need somebody who is close and I can trust to give me a hand. You've got the kind of ability and intelligence. It might interest you to know that a recent magazine article picks publishing as one of the ten biggest postwar industries."

It was Bobby who returned to civilian life first. He immediately proposed to his high school sweetheart Kay, then enrolled in Stanford and wrote to Dad. "It's where everyone from Pasadena goes." But Dad wanted to do something different from his brothers, so he chose the University of California, Berkeley, instead.

Both Bud and Dad made it home from World War II in time to attend their baby brother's wedding.

Mom and Dad on their honeymoon — 1950

CHAPTER THIRTY

My Parents Get Married
1945-1950

Dad received his Bachelor of Arts degree from Cal in economics and his mother bought him an expensive car for a graduation present. "He didn't go into publishing with Bud," said Bobby. "In fact, our mother announced to the family one night that she had invested in Bud's business deal and wanted everyone to know there would be less money to inherit for everyone.

"Your dad wanted to work with plants. He'd been interested in orchids since he was stationed in Florida. Our brother Bud knew about it and brought some rare specimens from the Pacific back with him after the war ended, which was the beginning of your dad's plant collection.

"After he graduated from Cal, a classmate of his, Patty Van Heuser, helped him get a job with her father. Mr. Van Heuser owned a beet-pulp plant in the cattle-feed business near Napa above San Francisco. I think your dad hoped the beets might lead into grape farming. He had this attraction to the wine country, which he called 'Napa, Sonoma and Mendocino' as if it were all one town.

"He lasted a year with Mr. Van Heuser and learned a lot about farming. Besides, the man amused him. Mr. Van Heuser built several moveable wooden huts with tin roofs where Tommy and the other help lived while they worked for him. Mr. Van Heuser had his own bulldozer and liked to ride around in it, rearranging the little huts. Often when your dad came home from working on the farm his hut wasn't in the place where it had been when he left it in the morning.

"Someone gave Mr. Van Heuser some peacocks that lived all over the ranch. They ate the snails and frogs, which are all over Napa, but you had to watch out because they'd destroy crops, too. Sometimes at night these peacocks perched on top of the tin roofs and pecked, resulting in a horrific noise.

"But what really made your dad laugh was when he told me about Mr. Van Heuser's hobby of collecting clocks. There were about 1,200 of them and he made sure they all chimed together every quarter hour. Tommy said the staff could easily tell when Mr. Van Heuser went out of town, because the clocks all chimed at a different time."

That would be the only time in Dad's life he worked for someone else. The following fall he moved back to Pasadena. "He sold that expensive car and just about everything else he owned and bought a small piece of land on the east side of town," Bobby said. "There he built a lath house and T.W. Ames Greenery was in business."

Dad began purchasing more rare indoor plants, particularly two slow-growing palms called raphis and sago. I think he considered plants a better investment than stocks and bonds. He had more control over whether they grew or not. "Those thirty-foot raphis are really valuable," he told me what seemed like a million times. "They only grow an inch a year, you know. And sago palms are one of the oldest plant species in existence. They were here when the dinosaurs roamed the earth."

If you were to ask him how many plants he had, you would receive a detailed inventory of each specimen. They were like children to him. He enjoyed the ritual of watering them each morning and evening, as if he were getting them up and putting them to bed. When I think of my father bending over to kiss me goodnight, I think of the smell of beer, sweat and wet dirt.

He developed relationships with a number of restaurant- and office-building owners for whom he designed and built interior gardens. He provided the plants and maintained them as a monthly caretaking service. This was before there was such a thing as automatic watering systems. Through the indoor landscaping business he sold some rare palms, but he kept most of them for himself. In spite of their slow growth, his collection began to grow out the doors of his lath house.

Down the street from T.W. Ames Greenery was a launderette owned by another young entrepreneur and bachelor named Al Coon. Dad went there to do his laundry and they started talking. A friendship began. Eventually they met regularly after work at a small bar on the corner. This habit continued well into my childhood. I remember being with Mom when she fetched him out of that bar. It had a red leather door with a diamond-shaped window in the middle of it.

Al and Dad didn't take long to discover they shared a love of surfing. On weekends and any other time they got the chance, they drove the hour and a half to San Onofre Beach with their hundred-pound surfboards strapped to the top of Al's station wagon. Saturday nights they slept in sleeping bags on the sand, right where today there is a huge nuclear power plant. The waves upon which my father used to ride his surfboard now cool the plant.

———◆———

Though my mother was four years younger than my father, she finished college before he did because of the war. After college she settled in Pasadena, where her family lived.

She'd been born in a *nursing home* in 1925 in England, then an eight-day journey from Chicago where Dad was a three-and-a-half-year-old toddler. Her Welsh mother, Eileen Thomas, was living in London when she met Mom's father, Prince Hopkins, dubbed by the London newspapers a "wealthy American socialite."

Like Dad's family, the Hopkins clan had lived in New England since colonial days. In 1850, Mom's grandfather, Charles Hopkins, left for California as part of the gold rush to make his fortune. He worked for a mint, which enabled him to put enough cash in his pocket to take a steamer back to Boston, hire a buggy to his hometown in Maine and marry his childhood sweetheart. Sadly, she died shortly afterward in childbirth.

A few years later he married Ruth Singer, one of Isaac Merritt Singer's twenty-four children. Isaac was not only smart enough to invent a sewing machine, but clever enough to marry several wives in various parts of the country, keeping all of them and their children from knowing each other. Charles started buying stock in the Singer Machine Company. When Ruth died in childbirth also, Charles received a few more shares. He was investing in other companies as well and in 1874 purchased a seat on the San Francisco Stock and Bond Exchange, established ten years earlier. He "watched commerce carefully, and made some wise decisions," wrote his son later. The following year, Isaac Merritt Singer died, and the year after that Charles sold his seat on the exchange. By that time he was one of the major stockholders of Singer, just as Levi's jeans and the elaborate Victorian dresses were becoming popular.

While working at the mint, Charles had met a kindly English jeweler named Samuel Booth who, with his red-headed Irish wife, had a pretty, golden-haired daughter named Mary Isabel, called May. Charles courted and won May, though he was twenty-eight years her senior. When they married in 1883, he was forty-six and she was eighteen. She quickly gave Charles his heir, my grandfather – Prince.

Prince grew up living winters in San Francisco and summers in Santa Barbara when he wasn't traveling around the world with his parents. After graduating from Yale he returned to California and became a socialist. During World War I, he found England more receptive to his views than California and there he met my mother's mother. So that is how my mother came to be born in England of a Welsh mother and an American father.

My mother lost her own mother at a younger age than Dad lost his father. Weakened by heart disease, Mom's mother died of pneumonia when Mom was eight, ending that part of her life when she was the center of her parents' attentions. My grandfather remarried and had another child with a beautiful but selfish woman who made the rest of Mom's childhood miserable. When Germany was bombing England in 1940, my grandfather booked Mom, his new family and himself on a ship to New York. As my father had done as a young teenager, Mom said good-bye once and for all to the only place she had ever considered home.

She told me later about the move. "Our ship had to weave side-to-side to avoid being detected by submarines. At night the stewards pasted black paper over the windows to keep the lights from shining out. As a fourteen-year-old, I found it all a lot of fun, but it was probably scary for the adults. I never considered myself American until I came here. My stepmother immediately shipped me off to boarding school in Marin above San Francisco and she and my father settled in Pasadena."

Probably from my father's point of view, my mother's entry into his life was well timed. She fit his prospectus perfectly. He wanted a wife, children, respectability and a big home with someone he admired. He also needed help with the palms bursting the walls of his lath house.

Mom's intelligence was enhanced by her English accent. She was very attractive and when I was young, I often heard my father commenting admiringly on her deep, brown eyes and elegant legs. She also had some money sitting in a bank account, which she'd inherited when her mother died. She was saving that money to buy a house.

When I asked my mom what attracted her to my dad she said, "He was an exciting and entertaining man. He loved life, was tall, handsome and very smart," she said. "And he loved to dance."

Besides inheriting my mother's flat chest, I inherited her taste for brainy men. Neither of us knew until it was too late that a man's being intelligent didn't mean he was compassionate. The household Mom knew was autocratic. Her grandmother, who held the purse, held the power; thus her nickname in her later life – Queen May. This is probably why it didn't concern my mother that my father couldn't negotiate difficulties in a diplomatic and equitable manner. My mother held the purse strings. It probably didn't occur to her to ask herself, "Am I happy with this person? Do I feel good about myself when he is around? Is this man going to be easy to please?"

Their meeting in 1949 was made possible by one of Mom's former classmates from Scripps, a women's college – small and elite – thirty miles from Pasadena. Mom had graduated a few years earlier and was working as a *Girl Friday* for a local jeweler on Colorado Boulevard. She lived in a tiny apartment with a young woman nicknamed Squiggles, a childhood friend from England. Squiggles was spending a year with Mom in America and the two often socialized with Mom's friends from Scripps.

One of them, Nancy Huggins, knew Dad and Al Coon through her family in Pasadena. One day Nancy suggested to Mom and Squiggles, "You ought to try doing your laundry at the launderette over on Altadena Drive. There's a handsome young businessman named Al who owns it. And his friend, another handsome businessman named Tom, hangs about."

In spite of having to drive clear across town to do their laundry, Mom and Squiggles followed Nancy's advice. Within a few months, Dad asked Mom out on a date. She told me, "Your dad had bought an older car, a gray Hudson Terraplane sedan. I can still picture him driving up in it for our first date with Rolly (the white Bedlington terrier he had at the time) sticking her head out of the window."

Dating in those days did not mean sex, even though sometimes Mom went with Dad and Al to the beach and slept in a sleeping bag beside Dad on the sand. Dating meant dancing at the Ship Room at the Huntington Hotel or the ballroom over the Civic Auditorium or playing bridge with friends. Mom hadn't had much experience with men. She'd been attending all-girls schools since she was fourteen and had dated few men during college because most men were off fighting the war.

I asked her how Dad proposed marriage to her. "He was already a pretty sensitive man, maybe even a bit too sensitive, now that I think about it," she said. "He was always saying little things like 'Someday I am going to ask you to marry me' to get my reaction. It was as if he was so afraid I would say no that he wanted to make sure of my answer before he popped the question. Then one day at the beach, he slipped his fraternity pin into a paper cup of wine."

"Could you see it?"

"Oh, sure. I knew it was in there. It was really pretty. Zeta Psi Fraternity. A Big Z with pearls in it. I don't remember him saying specifically, 'Will you marry me?' I just sort of knew."

The circles of society in Pasadena were as tight as ever. Mom said, "Even before our engagement was announced your Grandmother Edith had done her research. She knew I came from a wealthy family and I remember her saying to me, 'You'll understand him,' which I thought such a strange comment."

No sooner had they picked out Mom's sapphire engagement ring than Dad started making plans for expanding his business with her money. "He was more interested in getting more property and fixing it up than in our wedding," said Mom. "But the nursery your dad built was quite lovely."

They were engaged for a year. I asked Mom if she knew Dad was marrying her for her money. "Oh, sure," she said, "but I think we honestly loved each other. We did have plans, remember. We wanted six children."

First, Dad bought the lot next door to the nursery on which he built, also with Mom's money, a small office building. He planned three offices on the ground floor and our large studio apartment on the second. My parents' wedding was held in the garden of her grandmother's large, Victorian home in Santa Barbara called El Nido. "About thirty-five people came to the wedding," she said. The small number surprised me, because I thought Dad liked pomp and circumstance more than that, but it turns out Mom's grandmother and her pocketbook were in charge of the plans.

Mom's father put a Band-Aid on the situation by promising a large cocktail reception a few months later in Pasadena for friends after the honeymoon.

Dad's mother, Edith, and stepfather Paul were living in Honolulu at that time and didn't attend the wedding because Mom and Dad were taking their honeymoon in Hawaii. Dad's parents gave them the boat fare as a wedding gift. "I loved Hawaii. We had a very good time there," said Mom. "I really liked my new parents-in-law, but I thought it very awkward we were spending our honeymoon under the same roof with them."

One evening the two couples were sitting together on the balmy veranda looking out over Honolulu to the Pacific. Edith and Mom were enjoying a cigarette. Paul was puffing on his pipe. Dad, who never smoked, had just finished telling my mother the story of visiting his father in Florida during the war when Edith jumped up and said, "Oh, I have something to show you." She dashed into her bedroom, returning a moment later waving a newspaper clipping like a little Fourth of July flag. "A friend of mine sent this to me from Nassau. It's about your father." It read:

> *NASSAU, Bahamas.   Most famous fugitive is Knowlton Lyman (Snake) Ames Jr., retired publisher and financier, who sold his winter residence in the heart of Nassau a decade ago, moved to Harbour Island and hasn't been back since.*
>
> *Mr. Ames, who has been operating a chicken ranch on the island since his retreat from the social wars, told us that he prefers his feathered friends and monkeys to people, with rare exceptions.*
>
> *One of the exceptions is his wife, Dorothy, who shuttles between Dunmore Farms and a "Mademoiselle Shop" which*

she operates in a picturesque village.

The former publisher greeted us at the island's dock in a pair of shorts and a shirt made of multicolored feedbags put out by a chicken-feed company.

After transporting us to Dunmore Farms, he introduced us to his capuchin monkey Sabrina, his wife's pet simian Dearest Darling, two pet leghorns named Dynamite and TNT, a brace of nameless white turkeys and an assembly line of 1,700 chickens.

Snake showed us his weekly column in 'The Nassau Daily Tribune'" to prove that he still has printer's ink in his veins.

"The strange thing," Mom said, "was that after your father finished reading that article, he leaned over and whispered to me, 'Someday I am going to do what my father did. I am going to run away to some place and just get away from it all.'"

A bigger upset for Mom, however, was that Dad didn't seem interested in having sex. She was a virgin when she married him. His lack of advances, which made her trust him during the engagement, turned into a problem. She assumed it was because they were staying in his parents' home and didn't realize it was the beginning of a lot of excuses. "When we got back to Pasadena the situation didn't get any better," she said.

"Well then, how was I conceived?" I asked, for it happened three months later.

"In today's language, I guess you could say I simply jumped his bones." Mom said Dad was very proud of his little baby girl. He took me everywhere and showed me off like a prize pumpkin. "But he was jealous of how much fuss I made over you," she said. "He'd do little things to restrict the time I could spend with you."

"I quit my job at the jewelry store to stay home with you, but your father figured I needed more to do than just take care of a baby. He insisted I attend to the customers who came into the nursery. Even though we lived directly upstairs, it often meant leaving a crying baby.

"We continued to have an active social life, still dancing at the Huntington and asking friends over for dinner. In those days, every couple had a folding bridge table and a set of four matching chairs, in the way your generation has to have a microwave oven. Every time we went to a dance, a new song would be introduced, or a new dance step to master and your father could always do it. The ten or so biggest bands were recording their songs so the whole world could hear them on the radio.

"However, there was still no progress under the bed covers. If I tried touching your father, he would stop my hand and say, 'Oh, you are just going to make your moves again.' I thought I must be doing something wrong. It would take me ten years to visit a psychiatrist. I sobbed through the whole first session, saying, 'Why won't he touch me? What's wrong with me?' It didn't seem to occur to anyone to suggest he might not find any woman attractive. People then thought that homosexuality was fixable. I believed if I were a good wife, I should be able to help him."

My most recent photo of my dad

CHAPTER THIRTY-ONE

Taking Action

When I was living in San Francisco in the early '90s, homeless people were everywhere. It seemed someone was begging for money or work on every major street corner. Those sitting on blankets requesting help from passersby created a slalom course on Market Street where I walked from the bus stop to the college where I taught. As the Dow Jones average got lower, the number of street beggars seemed to go up, along with the level of guilt I felt for not doing more to help them. They reminded me of the limbless veterans I'd seen so many of in Italy when I was eight.

These people forced me to face the reality that my father could be homeless, though I knew he would rather lie down and die before he would beg. "Besides, he has money," I kept reminding myself. Still, these people haunted me.

There was a toothless old woman who wandered down the middle of Van Ness Avenue, talking to herself in an angry manner, seasoned with words I forbade my children to use when they were small. She seemed to believe evil forces were out to get her and paid no attention to where she was walking because she was so busy battling a demon in her head. I wondered how she got that way. Was my own father living like that? Or was he fine, just leading an eccentric life like his father, the Mystery Man, had?

I thought of an "odd" little lady my children and I used to see at our local market in Pasadena when my children were small. They called her *weird*. One day she was standing in front of us in the checkout line. Behind her back, my children looked at each other and pinched their noses. I noticed the lady's back zipper was halfway open but didn't have the guts to ask her if I could close it for her. Instead, I stood there calculating the inches of gray from her scalp to the dark hair, figuring a month for every quarter inch since she'd tried to dye it herself. Her outfit reminded me of my mother's admonition never to mix two plaids. She paid for her can of peaches out of a Gucci wallet stuffed with money, counting out the exact change with gnarled fingers, nails painted bright red, the polish badly chipped. When she left, the cashier smiled at her and said, "Good-bye, Patty." When Patty grinned back with a warm chuckle, I realized the score had changed. I'd been shopping at that same market for eight years, but no one there knew my name.

"It takes all kinds to make the world go 'round." Dad used to say.

Mounds of unconscious homeless, wrapped in sleeping bags, smelling of urine, huddled in the shelter of shop entrances on Union Street where I walked my dog in the early morning. The cracked and calloused foot of one these fellows peeked out of his filthy blanket as he lay snuggling a brown paper bag crumpled around a whisky bottle. Has Dad become an alcoholic? I wondered as I passed him. What's keeping him alive? What helps him get up in the morning? Was he ever going to ask me or my brothers for help? If he were hurt, would I ever find out?

Recurring and more frequent dreams of him began waking me at night. I dreamt I ran into him walking along the street. In another dream he showed up for Christmas dinner. In both he was agreeable, rational, and acted as if nothing had ever been out of the ordinary. Once he helped me solve a problem I was having with an art project.

In another dream, I heard a knock on my front door at my house in San Francisco. I opened the door to see Dad standing in front of me. His blue Oxford shirt was pressed. His hair was neatly cut and combed. I could smell the Old Spice. He spoke calmly and had a warm smile on his face. "How are you, sweetie?" he asked. "Will you show me your new home?" I invited him in and gave him a tour. He walked around, noticing how I'd decorated it. He ignored the fact that the rooms were badly arranged, which had bothered me when my husband and I bought the house, because Dad had so often preached to me about the value of a good floor plan. He walked downstairs and entered my art studio and then asked me to show him my art portfolio, a ten-year effort my mother had never asked to see. I woke up crying.

Movies and TV programs stirred up intense feelings I didn't know I had. If the story line evolved to a scene in which a father reunited with his daughter in a big embrace, I turned into a sobbing fool, even if I'd been as happy as a clam the previous minute.

Then a few things happened which pushed me over the edge. First, a friend of mine, whose father also had alienated his family, told me her father died before she got to see him again. That made me realize I'd better search for mine before it was too late. Also I'd matured from being a self-centered twenty-eight-year-old to a forty-one-year-old mother of teenagers. My missing him no longer jostled with anger and my worries about him overcame my fear of his rejection. I went to find the piece of envelope with the address of Dad's attorney at Reezer and Associates. I couldn't find it.

Several times within the next few months I picked up the phone to call information in Century City to see if there was a listing for the law firm, but then I'd talk myself out of it. "They won't know who I am. It's the wrong time of day to make the phone call. I just don't think I can do it," I thought.

However, there was a force bigger than I was. On June 8, 1992, eight days before my father's seventieth birthday, I was listening to a melancholy tape of Reba McIntire while working on a design project at my drafting table. Seven or eight sad songs lowered my emotional defenses without my knowing it. Then came the last song on the tape called *If I Had Only Known* about a man's dying before his lover had a chance to enjoy her time with him. By the third stanza, I was lost to hard, painful sobbing and felt as if someone were tearing my heart out. The tears ruined the drawing on the tissue paper taped to my drafting board.

I couldn't put it off any longer. It was time to go to Santa Monica and look for him. I spent the next two minutes thinking about my schedule. My children would be with their father on Father's Day weekend. Dad's birthday was the next Tuesday and the children would be home Tuesday evening. If I were going to look for Dad, why not on his birthday? Where to start?

This time when I picked up the phone to call information in Los Angeles, I actually dialed and received a number. The receptionist for the law firm introduced herself and said, "Yes, there is a Mr. Reezer here, but he is out for the day." I told her why I was calling. She looked in her list of clients for the name Thomas Ames, but came up with nothing.

"I can look in our inactive case file and call you back," she said.

A few hours later she did, "I'm afraid there is nothing under that name. You know, this firm split a year or so ago and some of the cases went with the other firm. I'll leave a message for Mr. Reezer and maybe he will know something."

It had been so long, I assumed Dad had been lost in the shuffle of the law firm's split. I believed I'd reached a dead end.

My next call was to the Santa Monica Police. Dad ruffled so many feathers during the period of owning the Chautauqua property, I felt sure the police would know him. "No," said the officer on duty. Then he asked around the office for a minute or two. "Nope, no one here knows that name."

Then I asked, "If you were looking for someone who might be homeless, where would you start?"

He dictated a list of phone numbers for homeless shelters, starting with the most likely to the least, ranging in location from Santa Monica to Venice Beach, further south.

I spent a couple of hours calling the numbers on the list. No one knew the name Thomas Ames, Tom Ames, Mr. Ames or even Tom. "You might send us a photo," they all suggested.

I went into the closet where I kept my scrapbooks on a high shelf. I have a lot of them. I pulled a chair in to reach them and took down the seven or eight books of the last years Dad was in my life and spread them out on my king-sized bed. After flipping through the pages I was surprised how few pictures of my father there were. When I came to my wedding pictures and saw the look on his face, showing so much love and pride for me, I burst into tears again and decided I'd had enough for one day.

The following day I again felt strong. I made a few more phone calls to the homeless shelters I had been unable to reach the day before, but had no more luck. Then I carefully took the wedding photo and another close-up of Dad looking over his shoulder out of the scrapbook. The second photo was taken at the little home my first husband and I rented right after our marriage. It was the most recent photo I had even though the last time I'd seen him was four years later. At a nearby color copy place I had ten copies made of the two images, both on one page.

I didn't want my mother or my friends to know what I was doing. It was my personal search and I wanted to do it alone, so when I returned home with the photocopies, I called an old boyfriend of mine in Pasadena who owned a boat in San Pedro harbor and asked him if I could stay on it there. It was close enough to Venice Beach and Santa Monica where the homeless shelters were to allow me to get up early in the morning and arrive at Norm's at sunrise, if by Tuesday I hadn't found him.

As I booked my plane ticket, I wished I had more time, but I didn't. When I found Dad, I'd arrange a longer stay. My children were leaving Friday night, my plane left Saturday afternoon, and I was returning on Tuesday afternoon, just in time to be at the airport when my children's plane came in.

Thursday afternoon Mr. Reezer called. I'd been so worried about having to tramp the sidewalks, I'd completely forgotten about him. When I started to explain myself, he interrupted. He knew exactly who I was. "I have a daughter, too," he said. "I think your father is just fine. He hasn't contacted me for a long time, but he gave my name to his landlord in Santa Monica to pay rent on an apartment. There is still money in an account here that he hasn't collected. My suggestion is to visit Norm's Coffee Shop very early in the morning."

We laughed, both remembering that it had been I, years ago, who had made that suggestion to his associate. I was extremely relieved to find out Dad was all right and pleased I didn't have to visit the homeless shelters, showing Dad's photo. I decided to surprise him on Tuesday morning, the day of his birthday, and enjoy the rest of my weekend sitting in the sun on my friend's boat.

Thursday night when I was saying good night to my son, I sat on the edge of his bed and told him what I was going to do while he and his sister were away. He liked these bedside chats. They dragged bedtime out a little longer and he had me all to himself without his sister around. "Mom, what are you going to do if you find your dad?"

"Well, I guess I'll approach slowly enough to watch his face. I'm not so sure he wants to see me. If he looks like he's angry, I'll turn right around and head for the door. If he looks like he's glad to see me, I'll sit down next to him and talk to him." I didn't confide that what I really wanted was a great big hug.

"What will you talk to him about?"

"I'll tell him about you and Amy. Maybe I'll tell him about that family reunion Uncle Bob had last summer. Mainly I want to know how he is."

"I don't think you should tell him about that reunion, Mom. I think he'll want to know about us, because you're his daughter and we're his grandchildren. He'll want to know who we are. He knows he's been bad, Mom. He knows he hasn't been paying attention to everyone and he doesn't want to be reminded of that. I think you should just wait and see what he wants to know."

I was amazed at how insightful a twelve-year old could be.

Norm's coffee shop in Santa Monica

CHAPTER THIRTY-TWO

———◆———

The Search Begins
June 16, 1992

The Port of Los Angeles is about an hour from the Burbank Airport where I'd landed Saturday afternoon. I wove through the import-lots of recently unloaded Hondas in my rental car. When I reached the chain-link gate guarding the Los Angeles Yacht Club, I opened the padlock with the code my friend had given me. The young college kid who was working for the summer as a dock-hand was in a hut just big enough for him and the little TV he was watching. He led me down a metal ramp to a wobbly dock where an open shore-boat was waiting.

The evening wind had died down as we motored a hundred yards among sleeping yachts. The *Ripple*, a forty-five-foot, blue-and-white catamaran, was floating quietly at her mooring. Dad would have loved that boat, I thought, as I hoisted myself up the three-foot rise to the deck. As the sound of the shore-boat traveled back to the clubhouse, I found the hidden key and let myself into the main cabin.

I was glad to be alone in the small, familiar room where I'd spent many happy weekends with the owner. I kicked my bag aside on the floor, pulled out a warm beer from a locker and went back out onto the deck. Propping my feet up on the cover of the motor which served as a table, I knocked the side of the cover with the beer bottle and said, "Skol, Dad. Here I come!" Then I sat back relaxing to the sounds of seagulls and clanking masts and gazing at a burnt-orange sunset that only smog on a horizon can make.

In front of the *Ripple*, a forty-two-foot Bayliner swung softly from her mooring. A red Sabot tied to her bow swayed up and down and its sail puffed softly on its boom with a small hint of wind. I thought about Dad's sailing lessons and again wondered how his personality could have changed so much from then to when I last saw him. How different was he now?

The next morning I hailed the shoreboat with the Ripple's foghorn so I could visit a nearby market and purchase some food. Then for the next two days I did nothing but catch up on my reading, sleeping and daydreaming. But on Tuesday morning my plan was almost blown altogether. I'd neglected to bring an alarm clock with me and by the time I realized there wasn't one on the boat, it was too late to do anything about it. Fortunately, I'd arranged for the dockhand to come by and fetch me, but he was a little late and then he had to wait a few minutes while I threw on some clothes. I handed him my already packed bags and quickly locked up the boat. The effects of the two days of relaxing started to fade.

The drive from the boat to the coffee shop took half an hour. I drove as fast as I dared with an eye on the rear-view mirror for cops. Once I got out of the car in Norm's parking lot, I tucked in my already tucked-in shirt, walked up the short entry path, took a deep breath and pulled open the heavy glass door to the restaurant. Flushed from hurrying, I stepped into the reception area in front of the cash register, feeling as if I were stepping in front of a grand jury an hour after my appointed time.

The restaurant was just as I remembered it when I was sixteen. Time had stopped here. I smelled bacon, coffee and buttered toast. The kitchen was directly behind the cash register. On my left and right were two small counters that stuck out from the kitchen like the square cogs of a bicycle gear. Two seats lined the edge of each square, enclosing pockets where waitresses were taking orders and filling coffee cups. I scanned the seats for Dad's kinky hair, realizing how gray it would be, but I didn't see it. Beyond the counters, on both sides of the restaurant, dining rooms contained rows of booths. I checked first to my right, then to my left. Even though the restaurant was nearly empty, it was a few minutes before I was convinced he wasn't in it. My nervousness eased somewhat, but disappointment settled in its place.

A waitress walked toward the cash register where I was standing. I'd put the photocopies of Dad in my purse at the last minute before I'd left home. So I took one of them out and got the waitress's attention. "I'm wondering if you can help me find someone," I asked, holding the photos out so she could see them closely. "I'm looking for this man."

Her eyes squinted at Dad's square, strong-jawed smiling face. "Have you seen him?" I asked. "These photos are twenty years old, but he would look something like this." Then realizing she recognized the younger version of me in the picture, I added with a self-conscious shrug, "One is of my wedding."

She studied the photos for a moment. "Just a minute," she said as she walked behind the counter towards another waitress. The second waitress, crowned by a furry little perm, looked as if she'd been caring for Norm's customers for quite a while. It made me feel better to see her kind face when she walked towards me.

"Are you looking for Tom?" she asked, her wrinkles showing worry and concern.

I didn't know how nervous I was until my heart leapt over my lung at the sound of my father's first name. "Yes," I said. "Tom Ames."

I reached over to uncurl the photos the first waitress was now holding, and the permed waitress took a look. "Yes, that's Tom," she said. "Who are you?"

"His daughter."

"Oh, I'm so glad. We have been worried about him! My name's Beth." she said and reached out to shake my hand with her soft and warm one. "Tom's been coming here every morning since I've worked here. One of the first to arrive, around five o'clock or so." Looking at her watch as if it were a calendar, she thought for a moment. "But, you know, we haven't seen him in six months.

"The last time Tom came in here was December thirteenth. He was awfully sick, coughing and pale-looking. We've been afraid something happened to him. In fact, the Christmas presents we bought him are still here behind the counter," she said, pointing behind her. "We considered calling the hospitals, but then we realized no one knew his last name. Nobody even knew where he lived. So we wondered if he'd moved away, to a place too far from here to walk, but then that wouldn't make any sense. He loves it here. He's been coming in forever. He wouldn't move without stopping in to say good-bye."

"Did I hear you say you were looking for Tom?" said a man seated near the end of the counter. I had noticed his strawberry-colored ponytail when I was talking to Beth and how he seemed interested in our conversation. So were several other men scattered along that part of the counter.

"He's her father. Isn't that right, honey," said Beth turning back to me.

"He just stopped showing up," said the man, his ponytail swishing as he adjusted himself in his seat to face us more directly. "I tried looking for him, too. We didn't know his address, but I knew the streets where he hung out. So I tried looking there. No sign of 'im. He'd sit right here," he said, pointing to the same seat in which Dad sat when I was with him. "He was always bringing in gifts for everybody. Now, there was a man full of love!"

"Yes, he brought in all sorts of stuff. Usually he brought in plants, but sometimes he'd bring suitcases that were almost brand new or books," Beth said. "We'd try to give him something for them, but he didn't want that. He just got so happy that we took what he brought. That's what kind of person he is. Just as happy as could be over such a little thing."

This information was amazing me. Not that Dad was still a part of the scenery at Norm's, but that he was so well liked.

"When did you see your father last?" Beth said to me.

"It's been exactly thirteen years." I said.

As I spoke, I remembered the last image I had of him, sitting on the curb after his birthday dinner.

"Do you have any idea where your father might be?" asked Beth.

I told her about my discussion with Mr. Reezer and how he believed Dad was living in an apartment somewhere nearby. "I'm sure he doesn't know Dad is sick or anything like that," I said.

"Why don't you call the attorney again and tell him we think something's wrong? Maybe he'll give you some more information."

I liked her suggestion, but it was still only six-thirty in the morning. I doubted Mr. Reezer would be in his office until nine o'clock. I decided to stick around for a while.

Beth ushered me to Dad's swivel chair. "Have a seat," she said.

"Does he ever sit anyplace else?" I asked.

"Nope," she said. "What would you like, honey? Breakfast is on us."

"Oh, a cup of tea with milk and sugar would be great. And maybe some toast and jam."

Dad's throne was at the outside edge of the square of counter seats. A well dressed man in a business suit sitting to my left introduced himself. "I'm Klaus," he said, giving me a very strong handshake. "I always come here for breakfast before work. I miss talking to your father. He's kind of the entertainment around here."

"And I'm Jim," said the man with the ponytail on my right. "I started coming here regularly every morning because of your dad. He takes an interest in all of us. Wants to know about everyone, what makes them tick, where they are from, what their backgrounds are. And he loves to tell stories. He's always full 'o tales about Chicago during the roaring '20s and the old days of Hollywood. He knows who married whom. Which stars had affairs. All that stuff. I keep thinking I should bring in a tape recorder."

"Sometimes he talks about his kids and his family," said Klaus. "Typical 'my wife turned my kids against me' stuff. I have a daughter I haven't seen in quite a few years, so he and I related on that subject. I think he would want to see you. Really. I got the feeling he is very fond of his kids. I hope you can find him."

All at once I felt encouraged and terribly sad. "I sure hope I will," I said. "Can you tell me more about him? What does he do all day?"

"Oh, he spends his day pushing around his shopping cart," said Jim. "He has his turf. I see him a lot up on Euclid Street a few blocks from here. He goes through all the trash cans collecting treasures. The guys know which places are the best for the good finds and which time of day is best. He keeps all his stuff in a garage. He showed it to me once. He has a lot of plates and flatware. And he's always bringing in silver things that he wants the waitresses here to polish, to see if it's real. He's talked about opening up an antique store some day. Said there was some money he was going to collect. He's also talked about buying some land."

"Yeah, I heard him say there's some money somewhere, too," said another waitress. ""

"He took me to see that garage," said Beth as she poured more coffee for Klaus. "It was crammed to the edges with stuff."

"Where is the garage?" I asked.

"Just a couple of blocks from here. We walked there."

Jim said, "Sometimes in his cruising around he's found things he knew one of us would like and brought them in to us."

"Thoughtful things," said Beth. "Once he read an article about something he knew I was interested in, so he cut the article out of the magazine and brought it in for me. You know, I agree with the saying that there are two kinds of people in this world: the givers and the takers. Your father is a giver. He is one of those people who is always trying to make the world a better place."

I thought about that for a minute. I knew she was right.

I felt as if I were attending the Homeless Persons' Breakfast Club, though most of the men weren't homeless at all. They just liked coming into Norm's early to see their friends. Klaus was an engineer, about sixty and married. Jim was a fifty-two-year-old ex-Haight-Ashbury hippie. Though divorced, he still kept up with his ex-wife and son living in Northern California. "I live in my Volkswagen van," he said. "I'm a beachcomber. I go to different beaches each day with a metal detector."

He looked too neat and tidy to be a beach bum. "How do you stay so clean?" I asked.

"I belong to a health club," he said. "I go there each morning, work out and shower. Then I come here. After breakfast with this group I meet another set of friends who are also beachcombers at another coffee shop. We compare what we've found the previous day." He pulled out a handful of yesterday's treasures from his pocket and spread them on the countertop. A single silver earring. Some coins. A piece of a spoon. Part of an old silver brooch. "I made six hundred dollars last year," he said.

I wanted to ask him the price of his metal detecting device, but decided I was being too practical. Instead I ventured some of my more delicate questions. "Is Dad an alcoholic, do you think?" My voice got stuck in my throat.

"Oh, no!" said Jim. "Those guys who are alcoholics, they're running away from life. They hide behind their gin and scotch. Your dad loves life. Sure he has his pain to hide. We all do. But he always comes in here full of cheer, eager to face the day. He has one problem, though." Jim looked down at his own hand, forming it into a scrunched hook. "He has terrible arthritis in his hands. Sometimes he'll bring in a bag of jars he can't open and I open them for him. But he doesn't complain." It seemed important to Jim that he was able to help somehow.

I leaned over to Jim and said very softly so only he could hear, "One of Dad's cousins told me he left the family because he was gay."

"No way," Jim barked. "He's no faggot. Who woulda told you that?"

"There's a lot I don't know," I was ashamed to admit.

At nine o'clock, after too many cups of tea, I asked Beth where to find the nearest phone booth. "There's one right across the street next to the Denny's there," she said, pointing. "You'll see it on the other side of the building." I said good-bye to my new friends. They all wished me luck, and told me to let them know as soon as I found my Dad.

When I reached Mr. Reezer's office, his executive assistant Kathy told me he hadn't come into the office yet. "But he's due sometime this morning. Why don't you come on over to the office and wait for him?"

With the morning rush traffic, the drive to Century City took forty-five minutes. I parked under the tall building of black glass and found the firm's office on the fifteenth floor. The receptionist told me to sit in one of two huge, black-leather armchairs. I felt out of my element until a smiling blond came in and introduced herself as Kathy. She walked me to a lounge, which served as the staff lunchroom, and told me I could make myself at home until Mr. Reezer came in.

I fixed myself another cup of tea, even though I didn't want it, just to give myself a reason for being in the lunchroom. Then I pulled out a novel from my purse and began to read, but it was hard to concentrate on the story. After a bit, another woman came in and introduced herself as the woman I'd talked to when I called Mr. Reezer from San Francisco the week before.

She wanted to know what I'd found at Norm's, so I described my morning to her. When I told her Dad was probably very sick, she assured me that Mr. Reezer would do everything he could to help. Then she left.

I waited some more. Kathy peeked in now and then to see how I was doing, but it wasn't until eleven o'clock that she finally had some real news. "Mr. Reezer just came in. Hold on a few minutes and give him a chance to get things organized," she said.

The next fifteen minutes seemed like fifty. Kathy came back.

She had a big smile on her face. I expected her to show me to Mr. Reezer's office. Instead she handed me a three-by-five inch piece of paper with something typed on it. I took it and looked closely.

2812 Arizona Avenue, East Garage
Santa Monica
If not there, try the V.A. (Veterans Administration) Hospital,
Westwood

I was immediately disappointed, partially because I was looking forward to meeting Mr. Reezer, but also because I was expecting an address with an apartment number.

"East Garage?" I said. "What does that mean?"

Kathy shrugged.

On second thought, Dad liked living in weird places. He'd probably made a loft out of the garage Beth and Jim had told me about.

As I set off for Arizona Avenue, I let my hopes rise again, thinking about what Klaus had said. "I think your father would like to see you."

Could that really be true? But what kind of condition would he be in? I imagined him in bed in his apartment, with newspapers strewn everywhere, and encrusted dishes in the sink, too sick even to walk to Norm's for coffee or help. Would he even accept mine? I wondered. Or would he be so embarrassed about his condition that he would send me away again?

LA Freeway

———

CHAPTER THIRTY-THREE

East Garage

In Santa Monica, 2812 Arizona Avenue is some twenty blocks from Norm's. I stopped in front of a two-story apartment complex. Eight apartments lined the left of the property, front to back, with a walkway along the right side leading to a back alley. It was quickly apparent that a sick man would have a hard time walking the distance to the restaurant. It seemed much farther away from Norm's than what Beth had described.

I checked the address on the curb twice, then got out of the car and followed the walkway towards the rear of the building, checking each of the number plates on the doors of the first floor while I walked. Skeptical about the "East Garage" address, I still hoped something looking like an apartment would have a plate with that marking. I finally reached the back alley where one would expect to find a garage. Four garage doors lined up on the alley, all firmly shut with dusty, corroded padlocks settled in their places. Returning to the front of the building, I climbed the concrete and steel stairs to an open walkway along the second floor. The plate on the first door read "Manager." The rest on the second floor were numbered as expected.

I went back to the alley to look around for additional entrances to the garages, or evidence of someone living in them. I didn't even see signs of Dad's potted plants. As the day began to heat up I could smell the sweet jasmine overflowing the fence. Turning around again, I headed back to the front of the building. This time a door was open at one of the apartments. A little spotted puppy started yapping behind the closed screen. I rang the doorbell and a young woman with a scarf wrapped around her hair came to the screen. "Can I help you?"

I still had the photocopies of Dad in my purse. I took one out, and held it up against the screen so she could see it. "I'm sorry to bother you. I am looking for the man in the pictures here. He's my father. I was told he lives in this building."

She squinted like the waitresses had when she studied the two pictures. "I've never seen anyone like that around here," she said.

My heart shot down the other side of the roller coaster. Dad was too hard to overlook. "How long have you lived here?" I asked.

"More than a year."

Nothing was making sense. This couldn't be Dad's home if this woman hadn't seen him in over a year. Dad was at Norm's six months earlier.

"You could ask the manager," the girl said. "His name is Curtis Rodriguez, but he works during the day and won't be back until five this evening. He lives upstairs."

I looked at my watch. It was almost noon. I needed to be at the airport by four so I couldn't wait until Mr. Rodriguez came home from work. Maybe I could get his work number from Mr. Reezer. I got back in my rental car and drove to Santa Monica Boulevard, the main street running parallel to Arizona Avenue. I'd noticed a Carl's Jr. with a phone booth in front of it.

I dialed Mr. Reezer's phone number and this time Kathy put me straight through to him. His voice was reassuring. "What you are saying is news to me, Mary," he said. "I don't know anything more about that address than what was written. In fact, I've never spoken to your dad about it directly, just through Mr. Rodriguez. I have Mr. Rodriguez' number, but I think it's his home number, not his work. Do you want it?"

I wrote the number down on the back of the sleeve of my plane ticket.

"Let me know what he says." Mr. Reezer said.

"Thanks."

I dialed the new number. After the answering machine beeped, I left a message with Mr. Rodriguez, telling him my name, that I was Tom's daughter, and that I was looking for him. I gave him my San Francisco phone number but also said I'd try to call back when I got home. I hung up feeling very depressed.

I went inside the Carl's Jr. needing time to sit and think. While doing so I ate a cheeseburger and drank a chocolate milk shake. Then, I decided to leave a note for Dad.

I drove back to the apartment complex, took another color Xerox out of my purse and sitting on the curb wrote, "Dear Dad, I've been down here in Santa Monica looking for you. Your friends at Norm's say you are sick. I got remarried and I'm living in San Francisco. I hope you'll give me a call. I also hope you had a Happy Seventieth Birthday." I added my new name, address and phone number. Heck, what would you have said?

Needing something to put the note in, I took the rest of the color xeroxes out of the manila envelope in which I'd been carrying them, then slid the note into the manila envelope. On the outside

I wrote, "To: Mr. Thomas W. Ames, c/o Curtis Rodriguez." A bank of mailboxes lined the wall under the staircase on the ground floor of the apartment complex. One of the boxes had "Manager" written on it. I stuffed the envelope into the slot.

My heart hurt and I was running out of time, but I had one more errand to do. Returning to Norm's I found Beth still working the front counter. I gave her my report.

Exhausted and hot, I headed back through the smog to Burbank airport, wishing there were someone next to me who would wrap me in his arms and tell me everything would be just fine. "Where will I look if Mr. Rodriguez doesn't know anything?" I asked the dashboard. "My father sure isn't making this easy."

As I sat on the airplane headed back to San Francisco, it started to sink in that I'd waited too long. It was possible Dad had moved and hadn't told Rodriguez or Reezer. But it was more possible he didn't have a home at all, just this garage to protect his possessions. If this was the case, it was likely Dad was sick and dying on the street somewhere.

Dad surfing, probably in Hawaii on his honeymoon

CHAPTER THIRTY-FOUR

Lost in the Computer

When I got home to San Francisco that night, it was too late to call Rodriguez. I tried first thing the next morning, hoping to catch him before he left for work, but I didn't call early enough and had to leave another message. Finally that evening, he called me. "I think Mr. Ames was here a couple of days ago," he said. "He left an envelope in my mail box."

Immediately I was excited. Then my heart sank again. "Was it a large manila envelope?" I asked

"Yes. It barely fit into my mail slot."

"I believe that's the envelope I left for my father," I said.

"Let me take a look," he said. I could hear some papers rustle. "Oh, I was mistaken. Yes, it says to Thomas Ames care of me. I thought it was for me from him."

Nonetheless, he assumed Dad was alive and kicking. That was a good sign, I told myself. "Mr. Reezer said my dad rents an apartment from you. The address he gave me was for an East Garage. I went to your building yesterday, but I couldn't find any garage apartment."

"Your father only rents a garage from me, not an apartment," he said. "It's in the back of the building. The rules of the lease say he's not allowed to live in it and there are no windows. But I did see the garage open when he was there, fiddling with his stuff. He wasn't living in it. He had it packed to the gills with junk. It's a big space, too. Enough to hold two cars. He used to keep potted palm trees next to it along the alley and I would see him there now and then watering them. But over a year ago, I noticed the plants were gone. It was all swept up, as if he'd gone somewhere, and I haven't seen him since. I just receive the checks from his lawyer and mind my own business."

I was back to confusion. If Dad lived somewhere else, why didn't he need Mr. Reezer to pay the rent on the other place? Could he possibly have won enough money from that lawsuit to buy something? No, that was too hard to believe. It seemed believable that he would rent a roof for his things but not for himself. I wanted to call Mr. Reezer right away to discuss what I should do next, but it was too late for that.

Lying in my bed that night, I wondered if I would ever find out what happened to him. Had he just been a stubborn old goat all those years, hoping I'd be the one to take the initiative and look for him? Or had he really stopped loving me, and wanted me to stay out of his life? On the other hand, what if he were dead? Who would know he had two sons and a daughter?

"This doesn't look very good, Mary," Mr. Reezer said the next morning. "Have you tried calling the coroner's office?"

I'd thought of it, but pushed the thought aside. "No. Do you think I should?"

"Well, at least we'll get some information, good or bad."

When I reached the receptionist at the coroner's office, I was connected to an Erica.

"I'm looking for my father, who has been missing since December 13, 1991." I was beginning to sound like a parrot. "There is reason to believe he may have died in Santa Monica."

"What's his name, ma'am?"

"Thomas Winter Ames."

As she consulted her computer, I could hear her fingernails clicking and was reminded of my grandmother. "There's a Thomas G. Ames listed here who died on December 29 in Santa Monica. He was fifty years old."

Since Dad's middle initial was W not G and he would have been sixty-nine years old, not fifty, I wondered if she had the wrong man or if there was a discrepancy due to sloppy bookkeeping and a bad judgment of age? "Can you tell me anything else?" I asked.

"Well, the report was filed by an Officer Brown at the Santa Monica police station. Why don't you call them and see what they know?"

I did that directly. Officer Brown wasn't in the office, but I could leave her a message to call me.

Right after lunch on June 19, I heard from Officer Brown. She sounded very professional. I gave her the quick rundown, some of which she knew already from my phone message. She was prepared with an answer. "We have no record of a Thomas Ames here, but we handed in a John Doe who died on December 29, 1991, to the L.A. Coroner's office. The report here says that one of our officers saw him walking along Euclid pushing his shopping cart. He seemed very sick. The officer asked him if he needed assistance and he declined. Two hours later the officer drove by and saw him lying still on the sidewalk next to the shopping cart. She checked him out and he had died. He had no identification on him. But the Coroner's office would've taken his fingerprints.

If he was in the service or had a criminal record, they'll be able to identify him. They should be able to help you. You should talk to the detectives there."

The emotions inside of me were going topsy-turvy. I knew in my heart this was probably the answer. After all, hadn't Jim said that Dad hung out on Euclid? It was only five blocks east of Norm's. What a lonely way to die, I thought. And what kind of family were we to let this happen?

The information still wasn't precise enough to close the door on my search. Tears were slowly warming my cheeks and an ache in my throat was becoming hard to bear. I went upstairs to the kitchen and fixed myself a cup of tea. I carried it across the room and sat on the bottom step of the staircase leading from the kitchen to my daughter's room, stirring the sugar long after it was dissolved, staring into the dark liquid. I was wondering how long Dad had been on the street.

Eventually I stood up and numbly placed one foot in front of the other to return to my studio and call the coroner's number once more.

"Just a minute, please," said a new voice. Then after a minute or two, "I'm afraid we don't have any information on a Thomas Ames."

Exasperated, I said, "Wait a minute. A woman named Erica in your department told me several days ago that there was a Thomas G. Ames, age fifty, reported to have died on December 29, 1991. Now you say there is no Thomas Ames at all. What's happened? Have you lost my father in the computer?"

"Ma'am, there is nothing here. Why don't you talk to Detective Hamilton? He's in the Inquiries Department. Maybe he can look into the file for you." His office was in a different building, so she couldn't connect me. I thought about how annoyed Dad got when he worked with government agencies.

My introduction to Detective Hamilton was made by his voice on his answering machine. It was friendly, low and grumbly like those crusty, old detectives on television. It was also kind, and had a note of authority and efficiency. This lifted my spirits a little, but I had to wait two more days.

I could not believe my father had ended his life as a John Doe. He may not have been famous like some of his ancestors, or as wealthy as he thought he should have been, but he was never a nothing, a nobody or a person without a name. Even at Norm's, the regulars called him by name, with the same respect that the grocery checker at my local market gave the eccentric woman who mixed two plaids.

Dad with his mother and brother Bud around 1926

CHAPTER THIRTY-FIVE

The Final Report

When Detective Hamilton returned my call he was as comforting as his voice had indicated. When I told him about the two different reports regarding my father's whereabouts, he said he would look into it. An hour later he called back again. "I think I've found what you've been looking for," he said. "There is a file here for a Thomas Ames, but it was labeled using all capital letters instead of caps and lower case. That's why it didn't come up in our database. The full name for this man is Thomas Winter Ames. Father: Knowlton Lyman Ames. Mother: Edith Ames Winter. Born June 16, 1922." With each piece of information I felt the hope drain out of me.

"That's my dad," I said.

"The report says here he died of pneumonia. You can get a full coroner's report if you write a letter to the office and send twelve dollars. His body was claimed by Thomas Moore."

"Thomas Moore, who is he?"

"I don't know, ma'am. I have a phone number here. Why don't you give him a call? The report also says your dad was taken to the

Lincoln Mortuary."

No one at Norm's had mentioned any Thomas Moore, but then who was I to think Dad hadn't had other friends?

"Well, I guess that's it then. Thank you." I said and hung up.

I realized I'd finally reached the end of the road. I had missed him by just six months. Poor Dad, dying all alone on a cold street. No children at his bedside. No friends to remind him that he'd done a good job with his life. No one even to report to his friends at Norm's that he wouldn't be visiting them at dawn any more.

———◆———

Until that moment, I had not told anyone in my family that I was looking for my father. I didn't mean to be secretive, I just didn't want to have to consult with anyone. I guess you could say I wanted to do it my own way. I was taking care of my soul, no one else's. However, there were five people whom I needed to include at this point: my father's two brothers, my two brothers, and my mother. I started with my brothers.

"I can't tell you how many times I had thought of doing the same thing," said my brother Tom in Vermont. "I just didn't get around to it. Just think, if you hadn't looked now, we might never have known."

When I reached Charlie in Buffalo, the first thing he said was, "I don't think I have one good memory of our father," which pushed me off balance for a while. Charlie was nine when our parents began their split. Whereas my reaction to the tumult was to be the good little girl, and Tommy's reaction was to get the hell out of the way, Charlie put himself right in the middle of the storm, acting up for attention. I hadn't realized it was so awful for him.

Uncle Bobby was pretty broken up to hear he'd lost his brother for good. "Well, thanks for looking, Mary. I sure wish there was something we could have done." He hadn't seen Dad in sixteen years.

When I told Uncle Bud, he sort of grunted, or mumbled something I couldn't understand, and then was silent for a bit. After a while he said, "Who's that Thomas Moore person?" I could tell how sad he was. He just didn't know what to do. He hadn't seen Dad for thirty-three years.

Mom was surprised and relieved. It wasn't that she wanted Dad dead. She was just tired of the drama and glad the sad saga was finally over.

Before me were questions most people confront when the first parent dies. There were decisions to make that until a moment before you had never even thought about. What do you do first? Do you worry about tying up loose ends, do you stop and mourn, or do you reach out and talk to somebody?

Since I find cleaning closets the best remedy for relieving stress, I decided to tie up loose ends and let the mourning take place as I went. The first thing we all wanted to know was where Dad's body was. So I dialed the phone number I had for Mr. Moore. The man who answered the line said, "Lincoln Mortuary." That surprised me. When I asked for Mr. Thomas Moore, he said "This is Mr. Moore," and then it all made sense.

His voice was kindly, with a southern accent, and he seemed, over the phone line, to be African-American and middle-aged. I told him what I'd learned from the coroner's office. "Oh yes," he said. "The coroner's office identified your father by his fingerprints as being an army man. If there is no family, as seemed to be the case with your father, and if a person has been in the service, that qualifies him to be taken care of by the Veterans' Administration. This means they pay for a proper preparation and burial. They pay for his coffin and for a mortician to take care of him and then they bury him. It's standard procedure."

"Did you personally take care of my father, then?"

"Yes, ma'am. You can rest assured he looked all nice and cozy at the end. We dressed him up and took good care of him." I pictured Dad in his wedding suit, though I doubt that is what he had on.

"Where is he now?"

"He's out in the Riverside Memorial Cemetery. It takes about three months before a brass plaque is made, but by now he must have one over his grave."

I imagined a plain wood box being lowered into a military cemetery with no one around. This all felt so cold and heartless – so matter of fact. "Was there a service for him?"

"Sure, ma'am, every Memorial Day and Veterans' Day," he said.

"Ding-a-ling," I thought. "Of course, that's what those holidays are for!"

"In fact," Mr. Moore continued, "If you have a copy of his discharge papers from the service, you and your family can go out to Riverside and they will give you an American Flag."

I pictured the military burials on TV when the uniformed soldier walks up to the seated family survivors and ceremoniously places the triangularly folded flag in the widow's lap. I certainly did not have any discharge papers, and I doubted they still existed. I liked this man, and was glad someone with warmth and caring had seen Dad for the last time.

After I brought Mr. Reezer up to date, he guided me through the next steps. I sent for the coroner's report for material proof of death so that my brothers and I would qualify to inherit whatever was left in Dad's account at the law office and any other accounts he might have. When I received the death certificate it confirmed that he died of pneumonia. It also revealed he'd had cirrhosis of the liver. "One too many beers," I thought when I read it.

The next question was what to do about the garage. At the very least, Mr. Reezer told me I needed to look inside it for a will. So we agreed that he would pay for the rent on the garage one more month and in the meantime I'd fly down and clean it out.

Army of the United States

Honorable Discharge

This is to certify that

TIMBER J HUBB 17 181 089 Corporal

4011 Army Air Force Base Unit

Army of the United States

is hereby Honorably Discharged from the military
service of the United States of America.

This certificate is awarded as a testimonial of Honest
and Faithful Service to this country.

Given at Separation Center
Fort MacArthur California

Date 15 February 1946

PHILIP H FONTANA
Major Coast Artillery Corps

Dad's discharge paper from the Army, 1945

—◆—

CHAPTER THIRTY-SIX

The Garage Again

Two weeks later I flew back to Burbank, landing on a Friday night with plans to return on Sunday evening. I would be staying with a friend in Pasadena this time.

After rescuing the furniture and plants from Chautauqua thirteen years earlier, I had reason to expect more of the same in the garage: boxes of junk mixed with family heirlooms, silver and paintings. This time I wasn't worried about saving furniture, except one thing, the drawer to the gate-leg table.

At six o'clock Saturday morning, I met the apartment manager in Santa Monica in the alley of the complex. I was equipped with a video camera, at the request of my brothers, and the apartment manager had brought a long-handled clipper. With my camera rolling, I watched him cut the arm of the padlock, feeling like someone between Ali Baba and a car thief. As dust and lint flew everywhere, we pulled up the wide garage door. The springs, which hadn't been stretched in a year, groaned loudly.

I stepped back in shock, trying to hold the camera steady to record what was revealed. Flat against where the garage door had been a moment before was a wall of crammed clothing, broken tools, the hint of a supporting bookshelf, rags and more lint and dust. I was afraid it might come crashing down on me like an avalanche. When I was convinced all was secure I approached for a closer look.

It was as if Dad had poked a hole in the top of the garage and poured the contents of a thrift store and a trash bin into it. Then an earthquake had shaken the contents inside. I could see dirty sweat pants, a broken answering machine, magazines and towels packed from one side of the garage to the other, from floor to ceiling.

The apartment manager looked at me and shook his head. Then he went off to work. I was left with my two days to clear away the eight-foot-high mountain. First, I needed a large trash container. Getting back into my rented car, I drove to my friendly phone booth at Denny's and in the yellow pages discovered a promising section on "Refuse Removal." A couple of calls connected me with Archie, a kind and energetic man who was to become my new buddy. He listened patiently to my story and said he would meet me in an hour at the garage and assess the situation. He would also order the delivery of a dumpster, the biggest he could find.

Back to the garage I went to await Archie. I stared again at the wall of junk, then tentatively started poking at things, unpeeling some from the wall for closer inspection. Dead center, placed at eye level and within easy reach, was a dog-eared plastic briefcase. A quick peek revealed some legal papers, so I took the briefcase and walked back to the front of the complex where I sat on the curb with the case to watch for Archie's truck.

One by one I pulled out and scanned the papers. There were legal documents pertaining to Dad's court suits regarding the

Chautauqua building and another for his injured eye. His passport was there and to my amazement, a copy of his army discharge papers. "Hey, I'll get that flag after all," I said out loud as I imagined myself having a flag placed in my lap.

More surprising were a handful of grungey yellow bank checks made out to Thomas W. Ames for an even $1,000 each. There were more of these checks inside opened white business envelopes addressed, "For Mr. Tom Ames, c/o Norm's Coffee Shop." But the whammy of them all was a single white cashier's check. I counted the zeros twice. $263,000.00. None of the checks had been cashed.

"Oh my gosh!" I said with a whistle to the empty street in front of me. My heart was racing. It was so surreal I chanted to myself, "I am awake. I am sitting on a real curb. This check is in my hand. This isn't a dream." After losing several minutes in a cosmic daze, I looked through everything again. This time I read the court documents more closely. The details were laid out about Dad's suit against the Harris Development Company. When he won, he was awarded $50,000 to be paid monthly in $1,000 checks. The second suit was a liability case against the City of Santa Monica for the damage to his eye when the police dragged him out of his Falcon. Dad used Mr. Reezer's firm to fight that as well and was awarded the $263,000.00 cashier's check.

But why had these checks not been cashed? Suddenly I became conscious of the fact that I was sitting on a strange curb with valuable loot on my lap. I quickly packed it up, locked the briefcase in the rental car just as Archie's truck pulled up.

I guided Archie around to the garage so he could assess the junk wall. "First we need to know if this is a solid mass that goes all the way to the back wall," he said. "Maybe it's just a barrier in front." I thought of the furniture barricades the revolutionists in *Les Misérables* used to protect themselves from the oncoming enemy. Was this Dad's castle wall in his war against his demons?

Archie took an old mattress down from the top of the pile plus some miscellaneous clothes and revealed a hole big enough for him to crawl through. "I'm going to go on in there and see what's behind this wall," he said.

"Great," I said thankfully. I was so spooked that nothing could have enticed me to crawl into that abyss.

He hoisted himself up over six feet of other people's discards and disappeared into the blackness for a few minutes. The wait seemed interminable. Finally he crawled out to report.

"You can walk around in there," he said. "There are shelves and boxes and piles of stuff, but you can walk around. The front is just a standing divider. It doesn't smell so good in there, though."

We developed our battle plan and set to work with a frenzy. There were to be three categories: the dumpster; a pile of things to keep and sort later; and the thrift-store pile. I knew we had to make decisions quickly, act on them and not look back. If something was broken, it went straight into the dumpster. So did all the clothes. But every box, envelope or other container had to be opened and carefully examined, because some things were hiding inside other things. All documents went to the pile for sorting later.

Most of the front wall went straight into the dumpster. Then things started to get more interesting.

A young lady named Sharon, who lived in one of the apartments, came out to watch for a while. She was a prop person in the movie business and loved this kind of stuff. At first she stood on the sidelines and talked to us while we worked. Occasionally she rescued something she wanted from the dumpster. Before I knew it, she was hard at work with the two of us. We plowed into the unknown, as if we were opening an Egyptian tomb. Behind the wall to the right were three sets of shelves like those you'd find in a restaurant supply store. On these were various lamps, pots and pans, odd sculptures and boxes of jewelry as if one day Dad would lift the veil and his garage would be the thrift shop he'd promised Jim.

We began suspecting Dad had been living there. There were used and new Sterno containers, evidence of cooking. There were odd pads and blankets which someone could have slept on, though no real bed had been laid out. There was still one mystery. If Dad was in the arthritic condition that Jim described, how could he have climbed in or out over that wall? Was it possible he'd been sick for months and unable to gain access to his home?

Left of center were piles of boxes of different sizes, stacked six and seven deep holding a vast variety of items. In one I found a stuffed teddy bear, a woman's purse, some jewelry wrapped up in Kleenex tissue, an incomplete box of dominoes and miscellaneous dishes. I opened the purse. Inside was more jewelry and an old wallet. Inside the wallet, again wrapped carefully with a tissue, was some money which looked very old and which I'll show to a collector some day. This taught me how careful I had to be. My brother Charlie speculated later that Dad was afraid people would steal things from him and that was why he hid valuable things among unimportant ones.

There was a box about six by ten inches filled with a pile of jewelry, such as I used to imagine hiding in the baroness's safe at the Big House. We fingered through the strands of beads, rings, broaches and earrings to see what was there. Though most of it was junk, we found a solid gold necklace and a ring with 14K engraved in its side, set with a small emerald.

There were definable collections. Stuffed teddy bears and ladies' purses were in abundance. There were twenty-plus boxes of china and silverplate flatware which Dad must have been collecting for the future antique store. He used stained and mildewed vanity cases with mirrors in their lids for flatware containers. Later, when my brothers and I tried to sell the silverplate, we sorted close to 250 patterns. When I approached the saleslady at a second-hand store that specialized in silver flatware, she looked at me as if I had stolen it. I would have suspected the same thing. Sterling silver was mixed with plate and stainless. Even spoons with the Winter family crest, many generations old, were mixed in with crummy hotel flatware.

The last area we uncovered was the far left corner of the garage where Dad had carefully stored family heirlooms I hadn't known existed. A large oil portrait of his grandmother Alice painted in 1889 and missing its frame was packed in a disintegrating box. Dearer and more fragile objects such as family photographs, Wedgwood china and books Alice had written were stored in plastic milk crates, which were stronger and more protective.

The milk crates were also easy to lift. Dad must have used his shopping cart as a shuttle to schlep them here from the garage Beth had seen. This area was packed more carefully, maybe when he first moved there. As time went on, he became careless, piling trinket upon trinket haphazardly towards the front. At the very end of his life, he just mashed things onto the barricade wall, another indication his physical condition was weakening.

I thought of a story Dad told me of two brother pack rats, the Collier brothers I believe, who died in their apartment in New York City. For years they saved every magazine and newspaper, creating piles that reached the ceiling. They burrowed tunnels in order to crawl around their place. I could visualize those yellowing newspaper walls. Now I was learning that the same Dad who had

told me that story lived in this windowless garage with his treasures wrapped around him like a baby's security blanket. He was
also the same man who used to tell me, "A person spends the first
half of his life collecting things and the second half getting rid of
them."

We sadly concluded that Dad's last days living in the garage
were not clean ones. The place smelled horrible. Rat poop frosted
everything. Dust, muck and dead bugs were scattered around. A
large can of foul-smelling liquid could only have been used for one
thing.

On a happier note, as we were sorting out the last corner, I
came across a long shape in a threadbare blue velvet jeweler's bag.
A pull-string cord closed it tightly, but I could tell with a quick rap
of my knuckles that the object inside was made of hollow wood.
With a yelp of glee I cried, "I found it. I found the drawer," and
brought it into the sunlight to show Archie and Sharon.

I've heard that the Jews believe that a person's spirit sticks
around for a year after they die before going off to the afterlife.
After this experience, I believe this could be true. I could feel Dad
lingering around me, like a ghost, trying to find me and show me
where his garage was. There's no doubt he had been saving the
stuff in that garage for his children. It was no accident he'd placed
the briefcase front and center for us to find eventually. He must
have known Mr. Reezer would be the link.

I finished my task as dusk settled onto Sunday. I'd rented a U-
Haul truck and a public storage unit in Pasadena for the *keep and
sort later* items and a future sorting weekend. Archie had taken
care of the dumpster and clean-up. Sharon had offered to call a
thrift store to pick up the items left in the garage, to be appreciated by future generations of junk collectors.

The drawer and I headed home to San Francisco that night.

My husband and I tapped a little drum roll and hummed one of Tchaikovsky's triumphant finales as we slid the drawer back into the womb of its mother table and hoped that Dad was watching.

The Bridegroom's Epithalamium, on his
Marriage with M. C. Feb. 15th 1699 — 1700

This day I count of all my Life
The best, because I've got a Wife
That's wise, & virtuous, fair, and kind,
Where all the Graces place do find —
This Day our King, whom God protect
Receiv'd three Kingdoms to direct —
Now if with great small things we may
Compare, then I may truly say —
That did not more his heart rejoyce
Than mine did at the joyful voice
Of thee for wedded Husband taken —
Till Death the Marriage Knot shall break —

Alex.r Dunlop
London April 20th
1693 —

An epithalamium written in 1693 by one of Dad's ancestors
found in the garage among junk papers

———

CHAPTER THIRTY-SEVEN

Sorting Papers

Dad's desire to prove his self-worth ultimately destroyed him. His battles with the City of Pasadena for control of the Big House, with my mother for control of his children and with the City of Santa Monica and the developer for control of his apartment building didn't make him feel any better. If it hadn't been for a fluke, or mystical presence, the garage would never have been found.

But it was found and now the mounds of papers, documents and dilapidated treasures were stored in the public storage unit calling to me: "Mary, let me tell you my story. Let me tell you what has been so important to me all these years. Let me tell you what I've been thinking about while I've been pushing a shopping cart around the streets of Santa Monica gathering treasures from other people's garbage cans."

I also still needed to search for a will. However, I wasn't able to attack the storage unit until August. When I finally did, Mom offered to go with me and was a wealth of information as piece by piece we sorted through Dad's voluminous history. We sat on the concrete floor in the hallway of the storage building, with the temperature over a hundred degrees and no ventilation, and felt as if we were in a sauna, sweating dust.

I'm learning, as my mother ages, that older people hate throwing things away. Dad kept every letter anyone had ever written to him, every art project we children had made him and every photograph we'd taken and given to him. However, these mementoes were overshadowed by bags and boxes of documents having to do with his causes. In one letter to the president of the Bank of America, Dad complained of his treatment by the tellers at the local branch. Letters and telegrams to city officials in Santa Monica and Pasadena complained about property rights, traffic problems, vagrants, taxes and utility issues. There were personal letters to individuals such as tenants and neighbors and for every letter he'd written, he'd made four to seven copies. Old letters had carbon copies. Newer letters were xeroxed. Nothing was categorized or filed. Often copies of one letter were mixed with copies of other letters. Just throwing out copies and newspapers whittled our pile down by three-fourths.

In spite of a lifetime of opinions, Dad left no will to indicate his wishes after his death. But one thing was very clear. Some force or spirit had lived inside his head pushing him, telling him that it was his duty in life to find a better way to do things and convince everyone around him that he was right.

A funny little note he'd written on a small piece of yellow-lined paper was a perfect example. We found it at the end of our sorting and it made us laugh. Written to the jail keepers while he was serving an eighteen-day sentence in the Mira Loma Facility Jail for being a nuisance, he was giving advice on how the jail should upgrade its dishwashing system. The note reminded me of the note I'd written to him and my mom during junior high school asking them to let me wear nail polish, shave my legs and go steady.

> *Jan 13, 1977*
>
> *Officer in Charge of Inmates, Kitchen, Mira Loma facility,*
>
> > *Dear Sir – I can do my job more efficiently and be a better assist to the dishwashing crew if I can report for my job of sorting the spoons and forks at all three meals at the end of "mainline" chow and be part of the count at the kitchen instead of at my bed in the barracks.*
> >
> > *If this is satisfactory, please initial this request and return with my property card.*
> >
> > *Yours very truly,*
> >
> > *Thomas W. Ames, 4189-312 A-2*

The day following our paper sorting I called Mr. Reezer to tell him I had not found a will. I also told him about the letter to the President of the Bank of America, and he explained what he believed had happened. "When your father received his cashier's check from the law suit, he took it to his local Bank of America branch, wearing his normal attire. To the bank he looked like a six-foot-plus bum. When your father demanded the teller cash his check, she asked for some form of identification, which, apparently, he no longer had. When the teller wouldn't cash the cashier's check, your dad got heated. So the bank kicked him out and, as you know, he never got the check cashed. He complained to me about it, but refused to return to the bank. That's how stubborn he was." He also explained to me that since the $1000 checks weren't cashed, the money had remained in Dad's account at the law firm. Reezer was sure he could get the money back from the bank for the cashier's check as well.

In spite of the fact that Dad's grandfather, aunt and mother gave up when life no longer provided what they wanted, Dad apparently retained his sense of purpose to the end. One relative said recently, "What's the point of living?" when it appeared she was losing her ability to walk. She no longer gives a thing to charity and she will probably leave millions in the bank behind her. My father, on the other hand, who was living on virtually nothing except a lot of hope, continued to arrive at Norm's each morning with presents in his arms and a smile on his face.

You're
in the
palm
of my
hand

A Valentine card I drew for Dad one year during college

—◆—

CHAPTER THIRTY-EIGHT

Coming to Grips

There were two more things I needed to do for myself before I could put the search for my dad and the reason why he left me to rest. One of them was to understand why he took his anger out on my brothers and me. I told a friend this, and she recommended an excellent hypnotherapist who turned out to be a beautiful woman with a sweet, calm voice with a New Zealand accent.

I told her about the time my father hit me on the elbow with the spoon.

"Okay," she said, "Let's see what we can do about this" and invited me to relax.

I lay down on the couch in her office and she covered me with a handmade afghan just like the one my mother and I had made one summer at our beach house. "Take several deep breaths," she said, "blowing softly out of your mouth when you exhale." I did as she continued, "I'm going to count slowly backwards from ten to one, and as I do, I want you to think of walking into a dark room, going down one stair at a time. By the time you reach the tenth and bottom stair, you should be very relaxed."

Within a few minutes of listening to her voice with my eyes closed, I was in a very restful state. Once she felt she had the undivided attention of my subconscious, she asked me to go back to the event at the dinner table.

I told her what I saw, describing Dad towering above me on my left and then seeing a flicker of light, which caused me to look up to find the spoon crashing down towards me. I told her it hurt and explained that I hadn't meant to put my elbow on the table. It was just a bad habit.

"What do you want to say to your father, Mary?" she asked.

At first, I didn't dare say anything. I didn't want to confront him and make him angrier with me. Then I realized that she was just asking me what I wanted to say, not what I would have said.

"Stop," I said.

"Say it again," she said.

It had felt good. So I said it again.

"Say it again, even louder," she said.

"Stop!" I yelled. "You're hurting me!"

"Now, Mary," she said. "I want you to change places for a minute and try to be your father. Think of yourself as your father looking at you. What are you thinking right now?"

The next instant I was looking down on little Mary. She had short blond hair and was wearing the green corduroy jumper her mother had made her. She had a horrified look on her face.

"Now, as your father," the therapist said, "what are you thinking?"

"I'm thinking that if Mary doesn't learn her manners people won't like her. I'm thinking that if she doesn't learn how to behave, she will be ostracized. I'm afraid if Mary doesn't learn how to be a lady, she won't fit in. She'll be common. Also I don't understand why she doesn't learn more quickly."

"And how does it feel for her to say 'Stop' to you?" she said.

"It makes me realize what I am doing. It makes me want to stop. I can see I am hurting her. I stop. I feel bad that I have scared her. I don't want to hurt her."

Somehow, as if the memories and patterns of my subconscious had been rewired, I finally understood what I couldn't understand before. Dad wasn't even thinking about me when he hit me with that spoon. He was thinking about himself. He was feeling his own pain and living his own fears. He didn't hate me. He didn't even think I was stupid. He was afraid. He thought he had a job to do and he was too impatient to let the lessons of life teach me in their own time.

The other thing I had to do was say good-bye. On Father's Day of 1993, a couple of days after what would have been Dad's seventy-first birthday, I drove from Pasadena to Riverside Memorial Cemetery with my daughter, son and our Tibetan terrier, Maggie.

Riverside is a desert area surrounded by red rock mountains. Though it has its own beauty, it doesn't look like a place Dad would have chosen because there is little foliage and no ocean. I obtained a map from the information booth at the cemetery entrance on which a volunteer marked the location of Dad's grave. Walking in and out of the aisles formed by the graves of former soldiers, we scanned the rows of brass plaques set in the grass until we found the marker we wanted.

THOMAS WINTER AMES

CORPORAL, WORLD WAR II

BORN JUNE 16, 1922

DIED DECEMBER 29, 1991

Men – all army, navy and air force personnel – surrounded him, as if after death their existence were defined by how they'd served their country. One knew that below every brass plaque was a military experience, but there was nothing to indicate that, beneath the uniformity, each man had a unique personal history. Nothing said, "This man died pushing a shopping cart on Euclid Street." That's when I knew it was my job to tell Dad's story. This book is his monument.

The cemetery was full of living people as well. I'd always thought of graveyards as deserted places, but that's not true at a Memorial Cemetery. Since this morning was Father's Day and many of these men had been fathers, it was especially busy. Some families set up picnics on the lawn and were making a party of it. Some brought chairs and simply sat for long periods at the grave. I liked the company. I thought if I came again I wouldn't have to bring my kids if they didn't want me to.

After standing by the grave for a few minutes, my children got squirmy and I wanted to be alone, so I suggested they return to the car with the dog. Then I sat down in the grass and had a good long talk with my father. This time he didn't interrupt me. This time he had to listen. This time I didn't fear he would say something that would hurt me. I filled him in on what had happened in my life since I'd seen him. I told him how I was already having trouble with my third marriage and how some men had been unkind. "Why weren't you there to defend me?" I asked.

As the tears flowed, I twirled strands of grass between my fingers, just as he used to do with my hair. I told him in no uncertain terms that he had been a lousy father those last few years and if he was up there watching, I wanted him to know that I hoped he would do a better job of looking out for me now than in the past, because I needed him badly.

When I had finished venting I felt a lot better. I mellowed a bit and started thanking him for the good things he'd done for me, such as teaching me how to take care of myself. I told him I knew he wanted me to be strong and independent and I understood he had taught me the skills to be that way.

Even though I could still hear him harping, "Sit up straight, Mary, and don't cross your knees. Ladies don't fidget and don't scratch. Try not to mumble and think before you speak," I could also hear him cheering me on. "Keep your head up and remember from where you came. You've worked hard and I'm proud of you."

I gently polished the top of the brass plaque with my hand as I'd often done to the top of the gate-leg table and said. "Thanks. I'm sorry I couldn't understand you bettter. I realize now you did the best you could. By the way, I want you to know I read all those papers you and Rosemary left for me about our family and now I know why our legacy was so important to you. I guess I need to listen to what you said all those years and start following your advice. I really love you, Dad."

That trip to his grave, and others I have made since then, have helped a lot to keep me connected to him. He's not gone. He's just not physically here any more. Everything he taught me, that his ancestors taught him, is still here. All the love he gave me is still here. And everything that I am because of him will always be a part of me and a part of my children and a part of all his great-grandchildren after them.

Suk's jungle in the Chautauqua building

CHAPTER THIRTY-NINE

Epilogue
2005

A few months ago I took a trip to Los Angeles for a conference. While there I took a long drive past the Big House property in Pasadena, then to Norm's in Santa Monica and the building on Chautauqua to see if anything had changed since I started writing this book twelve years ago.

The Big House property has been subdivided, just as Dad envisioned, and three large homes have been built on it which probably cost more than a million dollars each. Apparently, the frustration which led to his downward spiral brought better luck to others.

Norm's was just as it had been. When I asked the manager if anyone was there who might remember an old man who came in the early mornings, he pointed to Bea, one of the waitresses. "Oh, that fellow who always brought in gifts? I remember him. He was a really nice guy. What happened to him?"

Now they'll know.

At the Chautauqua Building I experienced *déjà vu*. Overflowing the retail space were raphis and sago palms, chameadora, orchids, dieffenbachia, and split-leaf philodendron. "Has Dad come back from the dead?" I wondered. "Was it all a big mistake and he's still here?"

I went indoors to find a jungle just like the one Dad used to have, but instead of finding him at the counter I met Yoon Hang Suk. Mr. and Mrs. Yoon came to America from Korea in 1980. He opened the nursery with just a few plants in 1990, the year before Dad died. "I don't remember any old man coming by here," he said.

The building had gone through some troubling times. In 1993, the owners shut Yuk down so they could repair the retail space. His plants suffered greatly, sitting in the sun during the year it took to finish the remodelling. No sooner had he moved back in January and bought a shiny refrigerator in preparation for February's Valentine season than the '94 earthquake shook everything apart. It also loosened the earth of the mud hills that surrounded him and supported the Malibu cliffs. When the rains started, the hills collapsed, covering almost a third of the building and most of the parking lot. The Yoons had to evacuate, but they had no place to move their plants. So they left them behind.

Seventeen homeless men moved into the shop and made their nests there. Were they old friends of Dad's, I wondered. They destroyed many of the Yoon's plants and ruined Yuk's brand new refrigerator. Yuk wasn't able to move back for two years and by then he had to virtually start all over again. The insurance helped the owners with the damage to the building, but Yuk didn't have insurance for his plants.

Today, however, his jungle is about as thick as it can be without growing into the middle of Pacific Coast Highway. It smells like wet dirt and concrete. To me it feels just like home.

Acknowledgements and Appreciation

First I have to thank God and his host of angels, many of whom I now believe are my ancestors, including my father, who looked over me, opened the doors, and guided me to the people who helped me bring this book about. I wasn't sure he/she had power over my life before I started this project, but now I do. It's been an amazing spiritual experience.

To all the people at Norm's coffee shop, thank you for telling me your side of the story and for giving Dad a dining room, a club, a family and your friendship for all those years.

In chronological order of their assistance, thanks to Barnaby Conrad III, my mentor, who waded through my horrible first drafts, yet still pushed me forward. I thank Faith Sand, who besides reading the first draft and becoming my publisher, is also my John the Baptist. Thanks to my family who told me their stories including my Uncle Bobby, my mother and my late Uncle Bud and the written memories of my great aunt, Rosemary Ames, great grandmother, Alice Winter, and grandfather, Prince

Hopkins. Thanks to friends who read, advised and supported me including Leslie Arnett Nafie, the Rev. Timothy Boeve, Douglas Clark, Gregor Goethals, Dr. Alan Ruben, Christina Small and Mark Neville.

Thanks to my kids who never complained about the time I spent writing, and even though they won't believe in me until they are holding a published book in their hands, they have cheered me on.

I couldn't have accomplished this without the professional help of my editor, John de Forest; my writing teacher and muse, Leslie Keenan; and historians throughout the U.S. who aided my research including: Donna Eilts and Barth Weistart in Minonk, Illinois; the librarians in Ashford, Connecticut, and Becket, Massachusetts; Max Davis, a Park Ranger in Boston National Historical Park; Mrs. Betty McMahon, a researcher for Ontario County Historical Society; Dave Carlson of the Pacific Coast Stock Exchange; The Society of Mayflower Descendants, the New England Genealogical Society, the National Society Daughters of the American Revolution and the National Genealogical Society.

Additional copies of this book may be obtained from your
bookstore or by contacting:

Hope Publishing House
P.O. Box 60008
Pasadena, CA 91116 - U.S.A.
Tel: (626) 792-6123 / Orders: (800) 326-2671
Fax: (626) 792-2121
E-mail: hopepub@sbcglobal.net
www.hope-pub.com

The typefaces used for this book are: Adobe Caslon Pro, Zaphino and Hoefler
Ornaments. Caslon, besides being a beautifully designed typeface and easy to read,
was chosen because it was designed in England (by William Caslon) and brought to
America, just as the author's ancestors were originally English and came to America. It
was the typeface used for the first printing of the Declaration of Independence.